THE SPIRIT OF WORSHIP

THE SPIRIT OF WORSHIP

The Liturgical Tradition

SUSAN J. WHITE

SERIES EDITOR:
Philip Sheldrake

ORBIS BOOKS
Maryknoll, New York 10545

First published in 1999 by
Darton, Longman and Todd Ltd.
1 Spencer Court
140–142 Wandsworth High Street
London SW18 4JJ
Great Britain

Published in the USA in 2000 by
Orbis Books
P.O. Box 308
Maryknoll, New York 10545–0308
U.S.A.

Phototypeset in 10/13¼pt New Century Schoolbook
by Intype London Ltd
Printed and bound in Great Britain by
Redwood Books, Trowbridge, Wiltshire

Library of Congress Cataloging-in-Publication Data

White, Susan J., 1949–
    The spirit of worship : the liturgical tradition / Susan J. White.
        p.   cm.—(Traditions of Christian spirituality)
    Includes bibliographical references and
    ISBN 1–57075–314–8 (pbk.)
    1. Public worship.   2. Spirituality.   I. Title.   II. Series.
BV15.W487   2000
    264—dc21   99–048593

CONTENTS

ACKNOWLEDGEMENTS

An author collects any number of debts, both personal and intellectual, during the writing of a book such as this. I must begin to discharge them, even if it is only in token. First, I offer many thanks to all the faculty, staff and students at Brite Divinity School who have been such stimulating conversation partners and supportive colleagues during the past four years. Special gratitude is due to Linda Hillin, Sherry Willis and Shirley Bubar whose provision of their invaluable secretarial assistance has made this task manageable. Denise Lester Dinkins has read the entire manuscript in her usual thoughtful, meticulous way, and her comments and corrections have made this a much better book than it would otherwise have been. And as always, I am especially grateful for the love, patience and support of my family. My husband, Kenneth Cracknell, provided his typically gentle encouragement, insightful critique and good housekeeping during the time this project was occupying so much of my attention.

PREFACE TO THE SERIES

Nowadays, in the western world, there is a widespread hunger for spirituality in all its forms. This is not confined to traditional religious people let alone to regular churchgoers. The desire for resources to sustain the spiritual quest has led many people to seek wisdom in unfamiliar places. Some have turned to cultures other than their own. The fascination with Native American or Aboriginal Australian spiritualities is a case in point. Other people have been attracted by the religions of India and Tibet or the Jewish Kabbalah and Sufi mysticism. One problem is that, in comparison to other religions, Christianity is not always associated in people's minds with 'spirituality'. The exceptions are a few figures from the past who have achieved almost cult status such as Hildegard of Bingen or Meister Eckhart. This is a great pity for Christianity East and West over two thousand years has given birth to an immense range of spiritual wisdom. Many traditions continue to be active today. Others that were forgotten are being rediscovered and reinterpreted.

It is a long time since an extended series of introductions to Christian spiritual traditions has been available in English. Given the present climate, it is an opportune moment for a new series which will help more people to be aware of the great spiritual riches available within the Christian tradition.

The overall purpose of the series is to make selected spiritual traditions available to a contemporary readership. The books seek to provide accurate and balanced historical and thematic treatments of their subjects. The authors are also conscious of the need to make connections with contemporary experience and values without being artificial or reducing a tradition to one dimension. The authors are well versed in reliable scholarship about the traditions they describe. However, their intention is that the books should be fresh in style and accessible to the general reader.

One problem that such a series inevitably faces is the word 'spirituality'. For example, it is increasingly used beyond religious circles and does not necessarily imply a faith tradition. Again, it could mean substantially different things for a Christian and a Buddhist. Within Christianity itself, the word in its modern sense is relatively recent. The reality that it stands for differs subtly in the different contexts of time and place. Historically, 'spirituality' covers a breadth of human experience and a wide range of values and practices.

No single definition of 'spirituality' has been imposed on the authors in this series. Yet, despite the breadth of the series there is a sense of a common core in the writers themselves and in the traditions they describe. All Christian spiritual traditions have their source in three things. First, while drawing on ordinary experience and even religious insights from elsewhere, Christian spiritualities are rooted in the scriptures and particularly in the gospels. Second, spiritual traditions are not derived from abstract theory but from attempts to live out gospel values in a positive yet critical way within specific historical and cultural contexts. Third, the experiences and insights of individuals and groups are not isolated but are related to the wider Christian tradition of beliefs, practices and community life. From a Christian perspective, spirituality is not just concerned with prayer or even with narrowly religious activities. It concerns the whole of human life, viewed in terms of a conscious relationship with God, in Jesus Christ, through the indwelling of the Holy Spirit and within a community of believers.

The series as a whole includes traditions that probably would not have appeared twenty years ago. The authors themselves have been encouraged to challenge, where appropriate, inaccurate assumptions about their particular tradition. While conscious of their own biases, authors have nonetheless sought to correct the imbalances of the past. Previous understandings of what is mainstream or 'orthodox' sometimes need to be questioned. People or practices that became marginal demand to be re-examined. Studies of spirituality in the past frequently underestimated or ignored the role of women. Sometimes the treatments of spiritual traditions were culturally one-sided because they were written from an uncritical western European or North Atlantic perspective.

However, any series is necessarily selective. It cannot hope to do full justice to the extraordinary variety of Christian spiritual traditions. The principles of selection are inevitably open to question. I hope that an appropriate balance has been maintained between a sense of the likely readership on the one hand and the dangers of narrowness on the other. In the end, choices had to be made and the result is inevitably weighted in favour of traditions that have achieved 'classic' status or which seem to capture the contemporary imagination. Within these limits, I trust that the series will offer a reasonably balanced account of what the Christian spiritual tradition has to offer.

As editor of the series I would like to thank all the authors who agreed to contribute and for the stimulating conversations and correspondence that sometimes resulted. I am especially grateful for the high quality of their work which made my task so much easier. Editing such a series is a complex undertaking. I have worked closely throughout with Morag Reeve of Darton, Longman & Todd and Robert Ellsberg of Orbis Books. I am immensely grateful to them for their friendly support and judicious advice. Without them this series would never have come together.

PHILIP SHELDRAKE
Sarum College, Salisbury

1. WHAT IS LITURGICAL SPIRITUALITY?

He was a young man of enormous wit and power, brought up in a wealthy Christian household just as the tides of fortune were turning against the Roman Empire. Fascinated by the myriad religious and philosophical options of the age, he had wandered far from the faith of his mother, and at the age of thirty-five he was sampling extensively from life's banquet, in all its richness and variety. But the story does not end there, and Augustine, scholarly son of Monica, has left us what is seen by many to be among the most moving and tender spiritual autobiographies of all time, the *Confessions*, which tells of God's persistence in drawing him back to the Christian fold. In one particularly startling passage, Augustine recalls hearing the voice of Jesus Christ, warning him against the temptation to think that his spiritual future was in his own hands. 'You will not convert me,' Augustine hears the Saviour say, 'like common food, into your substance, but will be changed into me.'[1]

In describing his encounter with the Risen Christ in this manner, Augustine of Hippo has placed himself firmly within what we will call in this volume the 'liturgical tradition' of Christian spirituality. He has taken it for granted that the words and images, actions and relationships which form the core of the Church's corporate worship are primary resources for reflection on the spiritual life. In this case it is the Lord's Supper, the breaking of bread in remembrance of the life, death and resurrection of Jesus, which gives rise to, gives voice to, a deep spiritual insight. Augustine is not *taking*, he is *being taken*; he is not *searching*, he is *being searched for*. He will be moulded into the likeness of the Risen Christ; he will not mould Christ into his own human image. He is to be Christ's food, just as Christ is his food in the Eucharist.

WHAT DOES IT MEAN TO SPEAK OF A 'LITURGICAL TRADITION' OF SPIRITUALITY?

In most cases when we speak of a 'tradition' of spirituality, we can be quite definite about its boundaries. They are usually set by the intention of a founder (or founding document) whose vision of a distinctive way of approaching the quest for relationship with God sets in motion a movement, an inclination in like-minded people to approach the disciplines of godliness in a particular way. While individuals and groups who have self-consciously identified themselves with a distinctive spiritual tradition may carry it forward and expand upon it, they do so within the general framework of the ideals that lie at the roots of the tradition. If we were to ask for insights about the living of a holy life from the Franciscan tradition, for example, we would know that the life of Francis of Assisi, the letters of spiritual counsel of Clare, the later reflections and practices of those who followed the Franciscan way would have to be taken into account. There would be a self-contained body of material to consider, and decisions about what was to be included and what was to be excluded would be quite easy to make.

To define the perimeters of the 'liturgical tradition' of spirituality, however, is not quite as straightforward as this. There is no single founder or founding document; there is not even an identifiable point in time at which we can confidently say the tradition was established. Even more difficult is the fact that there are very few persons who, if they were asked 'What tradition of spirituality do you represent?' would say, 'The liturgical tradition'. Indeed, those within the liturgical tradition of Christian spirituality are as diverse as Christianity itself. They are clergy and lay people from both East and West; they are Protestants and Roman Catholics; they are

Cistercians and Benedictines, Dominicans and Franciscans; they are Presbyterians, Anglicans, Lutherans and Quakers.

But they all have one thing in common: the liturgical tradition of Christian spirituality is constituted by those who say, clearly and consistently, that the primary source for the nourishment of the Christian spiritual life is to be found in the Church's public worship. As one Eastern Orthodox exponent of the tradition says, the heart of the liturgical tradition of spirituality consists in the willingness 'to understand the liturgy from inside, to discover and experience that "epiphany" of God, the world and life which the liturgy contains and communicates, to relate that vision and this power to our own existence, to all our problems'.[2] The liturgy, then, is seen by the representatives of this tradition as the basic food and general rule of the spiritual life of the Christian believer. 'We have given the name of "liturgical",' a contemporary representative of the tradition says, 'to that spirituality which . . . frankly adopts as its own the methods used by the Church when she celebrates the liturgy.'[3]

This dialectical movement between Christian liturgy and Christian spirituality begins as early as the first century. When Saint Paul encourages the Corinthian Christians to move increasingly toward holiness of life, he urges them to look to their common worship as a teacher (1 Corinthians 11:17–32). They are called, he argues, to recognise and to share in the Body of Christ in their eucharistic celebrations. But for Paul this is not only about a theological interpretation of, or devotional regard for, the communion bread and wine. He is quite clear that if the Corinthians fail to see that as a community they *themselves* are the Body of Christ, and if as a result they allow that Body to be broken through divisions between rich and poor, their relationship with the Christ whose name they bear is deformed, no matter how reverently they partake of the food at the Supper. This sets the pattern for all future liturgical spirituality: the common prayer of the Church provides both the model and the content of the Christian devotional life.

A SPIRITUAL APPROACH TO COMMON PRAYER

Of course, the liturgy itself is not monolithic, nor is it particularly stable, and so the proponents of the liturgical path of spiritual development will be using diverse sources for their reflections. One may be referring to the medieval High Mass in considering the nature of the Christian life, another to a Revival Meeting, still another to a Methodist preaching service;[4] yet all are certain that it is within the liturgical assembly that one receives the primary spiritual insight, strength, experience of the holy, and nourishment for godly living. Neither does liturgical spirituality encourage a particular methodology, but rather the development of certain attitudes which become part of 'the habitual atmosphere of the soul'. This type of spirituality, according to its proponents,

> leaves the soul full freedom of movement, that, following its own spontaneous interior inclination, it may open itself to the light of the divine mysteries, letting itself be gently permeated by that light, and may expand naturally and simply in the intimate, reverent relationship with the Lord.[5]

Indeed some within the tradition wish to go further, arguing that 'for a soul educated in this environment of spontaneous, rich, spiritual vitality [i.e. the liturgy], the rigidities of any method will soon be superfluous'.[6]

Even within quite stable traditions, various elements of the liturgy work in different ways to nourish Christian spirituality. As one seventeenth-century commentator says:

> [Christian worship] is a compound of texts of Scripture, of exhortations to repentance, of prayers, hymns, psalms, doxologies, lessons, creeds, and of thanksgivings; of forms for the administrations of the Sacraments and for other public duties of Christians in the Church; and of comminations against impenitent sinners. And all this mixed

and diversified with great care expressly to quicken devotion and stir up attention.[7]

Because of this, we will find that exponents of the tradition
are as likely to be reflecting on the spiritual meaning of one
specific element of the worship service as they are on the
liturgy as a whole. As an example, let us return to the *Confessions* of Augustine, where he describes his experience of
hearing psalms, hymns and canticles chanted at the cathedral
in Milan:

> I wept at the beauty of your hymns and canticles and was
> powerfully moved at the sweet sound of your Church's
> singing. Those sounds flowed into my ears, and the truth
> streamed into my heart, so that my feeling of devotion
> overflowed, and the tears ran from my eyes, and I was
> happy in them.[8]

So the basic perimeters of the liturgical tradition are set by
the boundaries of Christian liturgical prayer itself, by both the
diversity of elements within any given service of worship and
by the diversity of liturgical forms found among the various
branches of the Christian family.

THE LITURGY AND OTHER SOURCES OF
CHRISTIAN SPIRITUALITY

In the Preface to this series Philip Sheldrake says that all
Christian spirituality ultimately looks to the Bible for its
inspiration; and the liturgical tradition is no exception. All
representatives of the tradition recognise that it is around the
biblical narrative that the liturgical assembly gathers, and
from which it derives its motivation and energy. The liturgy,
in whatever shape and form it takes, always celebrates the
redeeming activity of God, especially as it is manifested in
the life, death and resurrection of Jesus, and it is because of
this that the liturgy can be (in the words of Pius XII's 1947
papal encyclical *Mediator Dei*) the 'fountainhead of genuine

Christian devotion'. Indeed, the reading of the Scriptures in services of worship is a constant reminder to the liturgical tradition of its dependence on the Bible.

The spiritual power of the liturgy is also rooted in the biblical emphasis on sacramentality, the willingness of God to make divine mercy and love visible in human history. 'Ever since the creation of the world', Paul tells the Christian community in Rome, 'God's eternal power and divine nature, invisible though they are, have been understood and seen through the things he has made' (Romans 1:20, NRSV). For the liturgical tradition of Christian spirituality the corporate prayer of the Church is the event in which that 'visibility' of God's nature and power is most clearly realised. This is echoed over and over again throughout the tradition. We are 'embodied', and God (having created us) knows that our spiritual lives must be embodied as well.

> For Christ has given nothing perceptible to the senses and even in those things perceptible, yet all is spiritual. So too in baptism, the gift is bestowed by a perceptible thing, by water, but what is accomplished is spiritual, the birth, the renewal. For if you were incorporeal, he would have given you the incorporeal gifts unclothed, but because the soul had been mingled with a body, he gives you spiritual things in things sensible.[9]

Thus, there is a specific biblical anthropology which grounds this tradition's insistence on the priority of the liturgical life of the Church for Christian devotion.

In addition to this biblical/theological grounding, many contemporary representatives of the liturgical tradition of Christian spirituality have found added support and encouragement from other more newly established disciplines and areas of enquiry, especially drama theory, the human sciences, semiotics and ritual studies. They look, for example, to specialists in human development to understand how the liturgy is able to become, in the words of the Second Vatican Council's *Constitution on the Sacred Liturgy*, 'the primary and indispens-

able source of the true Christian spirit'.[10] Psychologist Eric
Erickson, for example, gave the tradition the language of 'ritualised play' to describe the liturgy:

> [Ritualised play] is and remains basic for man's spiritual
> needs – or, to put it more generally, it is basic for that
> visionary propensity by which the human being in all
> subsequent stages restores a measure of feeling at home
> in the world ... to be centered in his sphere of living
> rather than peripheral and ignored; active and reflective
> rather than inactivated and helpless; selectively aware
> rather than overwhelmed by or deprived of sensations
> and, above all, chosen and confirmed rather than
> bypassed and abandoned.[11]

Ritual behaviour – of which the Christian liturgy is an example
– is necessary in order for human beings to be 'centred', 'reflec-
tive', 'selectively aware', 'confirmed' – all words which describe
human and Christian spiritual maturity.[12] But while the tradition may have found a new language to describe it, it has
always known about the power of ritual in the spiritual life.
We find much the same insight in the words which Gregory of
Nyssa (*c.* 335–395) uses to reflect upon the spiritual benefits
of liturgical ritual:

> We bow ourselves, therefore, before the Father, that we
> may be sanctified; before the Son also, that the same
> end may be fulfilled; we bow also before the Holy Spirit,
> that we may be made what he is in fact and in name.[13]

All of this is not to say that those within the liturgical
tradition have set themselves 'against' private devotions, meditation and contemplation. It is simply that these are always
secondary to and derivative from the corporate worship of the
Church. Poet and pastor George Herbert probably says it as
clearly as any in his poem *The Church Porch*:

> Though private prayer be brave a design,
> Yet public hath more promises, more love;

> And love's a weight to hearts, to eyes a sign,
> We all are but cold suitors; let us move
>   Where it is warmest. Leave thy six and seven;
>   Pray with the most; for where most pray, is heaven.[14]

Part of the tradition's insistence on the priority of liturgy over private prayer lies in the conviction that the liturgy is a total 'culture' into which people enter and are moulded. Others argue that the liturgy has priority over private prayer because the liturgy is a more 'holistic' form of devotion, involving body, mind, heart and soul.

For still other exponents of the tradition, the strength of the liturgy lies in its ability to make our devotion visible:

> For private prayer is only piety confined within our breasts; but public prayer is piety exemplified and displayed in our outward actions; it is the beauty of holiness made visible; our light shines out before men, and in the eye of the world; it enlarges the interest of godliness, and keeps up a face and a sense of religion among mankind.[15]

Others speak of corporate worship as 'soul food', necessary if the human soul is not to become malnourished. One Quaker representative of the tradition puts it this way:

> There is certainly a cumulative [spiritual] power where many persons together are fused and expectant ... Each one 'lends his soul out' to help the rest, and the corporate hush assists each individual in turn to open the avenues of his soul.[16]

A Quaker and an Anglican, whose forms of worship are about as different as it is possible to be; but they are in complete agreement that whatever common prayer is, it is foundational to the spiritual life.

THE SPIRITUAL RESOURCES OF THE LITURGY

What the tongue confesses the heart addresses.

Ambrose of Milan

We are quite used to thinking that the overall health of our spirituality affects the quality of our liturgical participation. The liturgical tradition of spirituality invites us, however, to think the opposite: that our liturgical participation has a direct impact on our spiritual growth and maturity. It invites us to 'live intensely what the Church is doing in her liturgy, applying our own spiritual activity to it and letting ourselves be penetrated by its formative influence'.[17] This is the overall vision of the liturgical tradition. But what, precisely, does the common prayer of the Church contribute to the spiritual life? Or, to put it another way, if the liturgy is the foundation of the Christian devotional life, then of what sort of elements is that foundation built?

For all those standing within the liturgical tradition of spirituality, the liturgy serves as a spiritual resource in six different ways. While different strands within the tradition may emphasise one or the other of these at any give time, over the course of the tradition's history, all have come into play.

a. A language for prayer and meditation

For all representatives of this tradition, the liturgy is our primary school of prayer, our first and best spiritual teacher. The prayers of the liturgy become models for the prayer which occupies the rest of our lives; the images and gestures of the liturgy shape our religious imagination out of which our prayer emerges; the actions of the liturgy give shape and content to our meditation. In addition, the liturgy as a whole grounds all of our prayer in the reality of the relationship with God in Christ.

The Christian educated in the school of the liturgy has learned the positive value of his life in Christ, begun in baptism, nourished and strengthened by the other sacraments; he knows the transcendental value of his vocation and of his personal holiness, directed toward the total perfection of the Church and to the supernatural embellishment of the Mystical Body.[18]

All representatives of the tradition would advise those who wish to deepen their spiritual lives to absorb the prayer of the liturgical assembly and allow it to become the formative principle for other forms of prayer.[19]

Of course, in order for one to become 'learned' in the ways of the liturgy, one must be diligent. A seventh-century representative of the liturgical tradition compares this with other forms of schooling:

> For if in the worldly schools of the arts, after spending a considerable amount of time, one is scarcely able to attain to a rudimentary level of knowledge, how much more is it necessary in the case of one who desires to attain to the knowledge of God and to be well pleasing to him . . .?[20]

And it is not only from the liturgy itself that we learn our lessons in prayer. We also learn our lessons in prayer from the other members of the liturgical assembly. The witness of the liturgical tradition of spirituality is clear and consistent that 'even in solitude, "in the chamber," a Christian prays as a member of the redeemed community of the Church. And it is in the Church we learn our devotional practice.'[21]

b. A pattern for the spiritual disciplines

> When true simplicity is gained,
> To bow and to bend we shan't be ashamed,
> To turn, turn will be our delight
> Till by turning, turning we come round right.
>
> Shaker dance hymn

While it may form the core of our relationship with God, prayer is not the only spiritual discipline Christians employ in the nurture of the spiritual life. Various other forms of devotional exercise are also modelled in the liturgical action, and over and over again the liturgical tradition makes it clear that the liturgy functions as a 'school' for these as well. Augustine, for example, often suggests to those under his pastoral care that they meditate on individual elements of corporate worship. In his advice to the Christian community at Hippo on the most effective way of reciting one of the psalms, he invites worshippers to 'walk in the footsteps' of the Psalmist:

> The one who speaks and ascends in this Psalm, aspires to the heavenly Jerusalem. It is indeed a song of steps . . . Reflect on what you will be there, and although you are still on pilgrimage, imagine that you have arrived, associate yourself with the unchanging joy of the angels.[22]

In addition to this form of meditative visualisation, other spiritual disciplines set within the liturgy function as patterns for the Christian devotional life. Fasting and other forms of penitential practice, silence, pilgrimage rituals, celebrative feasting, almsgiving: all these patterns of behaviour become habitual for those who allow themselves to be moulded by the liturgy.

The tradition presumes that much of this 'moulding process' takes place gradually, even subliminally, within those for whom the common prayer of the Church is the preeminent spiritual environment. An eighteenth-century representative of the liturgical tradition makes the point in a homily:

> [B]y set forms of public devotions rightly composed, we are continually put in mind of all things necessary for us to know or do; so long as they are always done by the same words and expressions, which, by their constant use, will imprint themselves so firmly in our minds that it will be no easy matter to obliterate or raze them out; but, do what we can, they will still occur upon all occasions.[23]

In this way the liturgy functions like any other 'culture': by continuous reinforcement of particular behaviours and by setting those behaviours within a community of meaning, the liturgy encourages fidelity. To the extent that 'we are children of the liturgy', says one contemporary exponent of the tradition, 'we cannot help bearing its image'.[24]

c. An arena for an encounter with God

> New wonder! Our mighty Lord gives to bodily creatures
> Fire and Spirit as food and drink.
>
> Ephraim the Syriac

The third way the liturgy undergirds Christian spirituality is by providing a context within which worshippers can experience an encounter with the holy. As a contemporary exponent of the tradition explains:

> Unlike those who believe that Jesus came once long ago and will come again in a future more or less remote, liturgy moves within the abiding Presence of God in Christ, the uncreated and creating Word, who fills the whole of time, past, present, and to come.[25]

For the liturgical tradition of spirituality, to enter into the spirit of the liturgy is to enter into an arena where the Holy Trinity is actively engaged in restoring and renewing worshippers as they make themselves available to divine power.

For most within the tradition, this is not an automatic or 'magical' process, but one which requires a willingness on the part of the worshipper to be approached by God. One of Charles Wesley's hymns on the Lord's Supper exhorts this kind of receptiveness:

> Draw near, ye blood-besprinkled race,
> And take what God vouchsafes to give;
> The outward sign of inward grace,
> Ordain'd by Christ Himself, receive:
> The sign transmits the signified,
> The grace is by the means applied.[26]

This sense of the liturgy as being the arena within which we encounter God is echoed in the Second Vatican Council's *Constitution on the Sacred Liturgy* when it says that the liturgy gives people access to 'the stream of divine grace which flows from the paschal mystery of the passion, death, and resurrection of Christ'.[27]

d. Signs, symbols and rituals by which to express the relationship with God

Our relationship with God is complex, multifaceted, and very often beyond our ability to express or describe. For the liturgical tradition, the liturgy becomes, in the words of one contemporary theologian, our 'primary speech' about that relationship.[28] The liturgy allows Christians the opportunity to praise God, to thank God, to offer themselves to God. It gives expression to the deepest human longings for God. In the corporate prayer of the Church worshippers are able to voice their lament, their exultation, their anxiety, their guilt and their desire. As Evelyn Underhill, an exponent of the liturgical tradition from the first half of the twentieth-century, says:

> The whole poetry of man's relation to the unseen Love is hidden in the Liturgy: with its roots in history, its eyes set upon Eternity, its mingled outbursts of praise and supplication, penitence and delight, it encloses and carries forward the devotion of the individual soul, lost in that mighty melody.[29]

All exponents of the liturgical tradition of spirituality would agree that it is in the liturgy that human beings are able to be most open before and vulnerable to God. Because of this, love and faith reach their highest form of expression.

Once again, we are 'schooled' by this experience of being able to say before God all that the human heart contains. This is because in expressing our own love of God in the liturgy we are set within the totality of the Christian experience of relationship with God, past and present, and we look forward to the consummation of that relationship at the end of time. Thus, even when we are weak, incoherent or rendered silent, we are still carried onward toward God by the liturgy:

> The liturgy, the dwelling-place of present and remembered encounter with the living God, itself begins to think and speak for the assembly, and turns wholly into music, not in the sense of outward, audible sounds, but by virtue of the power and momentum of its inward flow. Then, like the current of a mighty river polishing stones and turning wheels by its very movement, the flow of liturgical worship creates in passing and by the flow of its own laws, cadence and rhythm, and countless other forms and formations, something still more important and until now undiscovered, unconsidered, and unnamed.[30]

Because the liturgy has a way, in the words of George Herbert, of 'opening the soul's most subtle rooms',[31] there is a kind of radical honesty that it draws forth from us, and because of this to speak liturgically of our experience of God is inevitably to deepen it.

e. A model for the Christian life and community

Philip Sheldrake also speaks of spirituality as something which concerns both the relationship with God and the living out of that relationship in the world. For the liturgical tradition, the shape and content of Christian liturgical prayer is the pattern for the shape and content of that 'living out' by providing models for human relationships within and outside of the community of faith. Through visions of genuine holiness, through acts of reconciliation with God and other human beings, and images of the future of the world and its contents, the liturgy reorders all our dealings with others. As Gordon Lathrop, a contemporary Lutheran representative of the tradition, expresses it:

Assembly, Sunday, bath, word, meal, prayers and ministries are called upon [as Luther said] to 'speak and drive
Christ.' Word and sign in the assembly thereby cast a new
light on the world, suggest meanings where there had
been only meaninglessness, propose justice, and relativize
structures that threaten full human life before God. They
do so surely, graciously, without recruiting us for any
ideology.[32]

Regis Duffy, a Roman Catholic, gives a trenchant example
of this:

At the beginning of every Eucharist members of the community are called to serious accountability and
recommitment when, after some reflection, they pray, 'I
confess to Almighty God,' in one form or another. Above
all we must learn again to ask forgiveness in non-ritual
situations of home life, at work, and in school, and the
community must learn to ask forgiveness when it has
failed an individual.[33]

f. Strength in times of spiritual crisis

You must have faith that everything the Holy Church
does, reads, or sings, and all her sacraments, strengthen
you spiritually.

The Ancrene Wisse[34]

From its very beginnings in the first century, the liturgical
tradition has been clear that whatever else it may be, the
liturgy is first and foremost a source of spiritual sustenance
in times of temptation, trial and torment. Chrysostom called
it a 'hospital and a harbour', others a sword, a suit of armour,
and a shield. The earliest representatives of the tradition
believed that wherever God's grace was particularly present,
there too was the Devil lurking, waiting to confound the works
of righteousness. And since God was particularly present wherever Christians gathered for prayer, so too was some protection

from the forces of evil especially needed. For John Chrysostom, in addition to the weapons provided in baptism, in the Lord's Supper '[Christ] has also prepared a food which is more powerful than any armor'.

> If the devil merely sees you returning from the Master's banquet, he flees faster than any wind, as if he had seen a lion breathing forth flames from his mouth ... If you show him a tongue stained with the precious blood, he will not be able to make a stand; if you show him your mouth all crimsoned and ruddy, cowardly beast that he is, he will run away.

So, Chrysostom exhorts his hearers, 'Let us come away from the table like fire-breathing lions of whom the devil is afraid!'[35]

But even if they do not use such 'infernal' imagery, all representatives of the tradition have remarked on the power of the liturgy to heal and to sustain. At the other end of the spectrum, the peaceable Robert Barclay, the great theologian of the Society of Friends, gives an autobiographical witness to this power:

> For when I came into the silent assemblies of God's people, I felt a secret power among them which touched my heart, and as I gave way unto it, I found the evil weakening in me and the good raised up. And so I became thus knit and united unto them, hungering more and more after the increase of this power and life.[36]

Often it is the quietest voices in the tradition which sound this note, those who are marginalised, oppressed, shut out of the power-structures of society. For these especially, common prayer is the 'balm in Gilead', the medicine for the 'sin-sick soul', and the liturgical assembly is the infirmary within which that medicine is administered.

WHAT LITURGICAL SPIRITUALITY IS NOT

> Each person is a 'liturgy' in the original sense of the word
> leitourgia – 'a publicly manifest expression of God in
> Christ to the world.'
>
> Norman Pittenger[37]

Despite this rather 'functional' approach to the spiritual
resources of the liturgy, the liturgical tradition is not preoccu-
pied with how the liturgy 'works' or 'what it means', but rather
how it nourishes, sustains, influences, enriches and enlivens
the relationship between the Christian believer and God. But
it is always unpredictable. As Kathleen Norris told herself
when she was struggling with the rhythms of Benedictine daily
worship, trying to 'think her way into' the sense of it, 'Stop
making sense, I'd say to myself; sit in these words, this silence
for awhile. Sing the psalm and see what happens.'[38]

Neither are the periodic celebrations of the Christian liturgy
seen by the tradition to be spiritual 'pitstops' for individual
souls, but essential nourishment for the mission of the Church
for the sake of the world's redemption. The liturgy is not simply
a 'solution', not the answer to some intellectual conundrum,
but a gift. And it is only when this gift is joyfully accepted
that it becomes a solution to life's eternal questions. 'Or, it
may be,' as Alexander Schmemann says, 'that the joy of that
gift makes both the problem and the solution unnecessary,
irrelevant.'[39] The deepest desire of those within the liturgical
tradition is that all of us, as individuals and as communities
of faith, become 'liturgical people'.[40]

> But how does one do this? Surely not so much by striving
> and struggling in a moral fashion towards some supposed
> perfection; rather, the man who is formed by and informed
> with the spirit of the liturgy comes to that specifically
> Christian mode of existence by continuing exposure to God
> and to God's activity as these are made available to him
> through his participation in the Divine Action that in its
> humanly conditioned expression *is* the liturgy.[41]

To become the liturgy we celebrate: from its deepest roots in the New Testament to its most recent representative, the tradition is unequivocal in its insistence that this is the goal of the Christian life. Many contemporary exponents of liturgical spirituality make this point by quoting Feuerbach's famous dictum: 'You are what you eat', and then go on to speak of human beings as 'hungry for God' and of the liturgy as the 'food' which fills that hunger, making us what we are. 'To eat is still something more than to maintain bodily functions. People may not understand what that "something more" is, but they nonetheless desire to celebrate it. They are still hungry for sacramental life.'[42] And of course 1,500 years earlier, Augustine expresses the very same sentiment employing his magnificent homiletical rhetoric:

> Remember that bread is not made from one grain, but from many. When you were exorcised [before baptism] you were, after a fashion, milled. When you were baptized you were moistened. When you received the fire of the Holy Spirit you were baked. Be what you see; receive what you are.[43]

'Be what you see; receive what you are.' In these words Augustine sums up both the form and the substance of liturgical spirituality.

THE TASK OF THIS VOLUME

It must be said that most of the people represented in this volume are better known for other aspects of their work. They are Christian thinkers and pastors, ethicists and reformers. But even within these roles, for each one the liturgy is central. Some would be recognised as 'liturgical theologians',[44] who understand the Church's expression of faith embodied in the liturgy to be a primary source for the development of Christian doctrine. Some are notable ecumenists, with a deep investment in ensuring that corporate worship serves as a source of unity rather than a source of division between and among estranged

branches of the one Christian family. Others are known princi-
pally as liturgical change-agents, whose deep conviction about
the centrality of common prayer to the nourishment of the
spiritual life led them to advocate sometimes-radical modifi-
cations in the shape and content of the liturgy. Not a few of
these theologians, pastors and reformers have been willing to
risk lives for the Christian faith, and at the moment of their
death found in the liturgy a wealth of words and images to
express the meaning of their sacrifice. Although people in all
of these categories are well represented here – Augustine of
Hippo and Martin Luther, Ignatius of Antioch and Deitrich
Bonhoeffer, for example – neither theology nor reform nor
persecution is the focus of this volume.

By the same token, not all exponents of the liturgical tradition by any means are represented here. This volume is
intended as an introduction to the basic approaches and modes
of thought within this tradition, rather than an exhaustive
survey. And of course, like other traditions of spirituality, the
true strength of the liturgical tradition lies not simply in
the eloquence of the great theologians who represent it, but
in the patient devotion of generation after generation of
ordinary men, women and children, who quite naturally
describe their spiritual lives in liturgical terms, and who have
found in the worship of the Church an irreplaceable source of
spiritual strength and renewal.[45] These are the 'hidden voices'
of liturgical spirituality, whose testimony should not be overlooked. In addition, as with other traditions of Christian
spirituality, there is a natural waxing and waning of the force
of the liturgical tradition, and not all periods of history are
equally represented here. The link between liturgy and spirituality is perhaps most difficult to discern when the liturgy is
used for other than purely religious ends.[46]

Although the liturgical tradition is most acutely aware of
the fact that there are very particular conditions under
which the relationship between liturgy and spirituality is con-
fected, I have left much of the tradition's critique of both rites

and worshippers for another occasion. So observations like those of Gerald Vann are probably under-represented:

> It is far from sufficient to herd people into church; on the contrary, if once they are presented with vapid statues and vapid sermons, and are made to sing mindless yearnings to flee from the wicked world and rest in a somewhat negative and superlatively comfortable deity, their instincts are in fact being set precisely in the wrong direction: they are being suggested into subhumanity instead of helped into divinity.[47]

What we are left with, then, is perhaps a more 'affirmative' view of the tradition than some would offer, but it is hoped that this will not be looked upon as a serious distortion.

Although I have drawn from nearly every century of the Church's life for this study, and many of the testimonies are ancient, appropriating antique liturgical forms in their reflections, the categories I have used to organise them are modern ones, attempting to answer the question: 'How can the liturgical tradition of spirituality become a resource for the *contemporary* spiritual quest?' Can a generation of people who have moved into a new millennium, bringing with them myriad questions about the meaning of their own lives, about the future of the human race and of the planet we inhabit, tap into this particular wellspring of imagery and energy for their relationship with God?

To this end I have established six categories, and am asking within each one how the liturgical tradition of spirituality approaches its problems and possibilities. In every age, but perhaps more acutely in our own, they present us with significant spiritual challenges. They are questions about living and dying, about being with others and living ethical lives, about locating ourselves in time and space, about who we are and how we are to see our relationship with the God who made and redeemed us. Throughout its history, the liturgical tradition of Christian spirituality has given considerable attention to all of these, and they seemed to set a fitting agenda

for an introduction to the tradition. Can the liturgical tradition
of spirituality become a resource for the contemporary spiritual quest? The reader is invited to decide.

2 REVEALING OUR IDENTITY AND VOCATION

Without worship you shrink, it is as brutal as that.

Peter Schaeffer, *Equus*

Priesthood should be our calling
Even if we do not wear liturgical garments.
We should publicly testify to the divine glory
With words, music, dance, and every sign.

Czeslaw Milosz[1]

THE CONTEMPORARY PROBLEM

It seems so natural to us now: we grow up, get an education, find a suitable job, choose a life partner and a place to live, decide about children, plan for retirement. But the ability to make these kinds of decisions for ourselves is a relatively recent social phenomenon. In the past, traditional structures of class, race, gender and economic status generally bound people to certain courses of action and patterns of relationship. Throughout most of Christian history, for rich and poor alike, personal preference played very little part in one's state in life: as often as not, the sons of labourers grew up to be labourers; the daughters of merchants grew up to become the wives of merchants; the children of Londoners grew up to live in London. If there is any single change which modernity has brought about, the sense that we can actively decide among many equally legitimate possible courses of action may be the most significant. We sum up this change whenever we use the term 'lifestyle'.

While this widening of options has clearly led to a greater sense of individual freedom and autonomy, it has also created what might be described as a 'crisis of vocation' for many of us. In the midst of innumerable choices, and without a clear sense of where our own life-path 'fits' within the overall scheme of things, finding a clear direction is more difficult. For many, it creates what Charles Peguy called a 'kingdom of incurable anxiety'. If all life choices are equally valid, and depend only upon what I might want or need at a particular point, and if it all might have been different had I made different choices, I will have serious difficulty determining where my life contributes to some 'eternal plan'. In a sense I have traded in one form of bondage for another: the bondage of social determinism for the bondage of aimless desire.

While individual choice about whether to adopt a particular path or state of life is relatively new to us, historically most traditions of Christian spirituality have seen one's state in life as having positive spiritual value. Many of our Christian forebears were convinced that God places each person in a particular set of circumstances, and it is precisely within those circumstances that we seek to 'work out our salvation in fear and trembling' (Philippians 2:12). Martin Luther, for example, spoke of three '*Stunde*' or states of life, and suggested that whether you were a priest, a government official, or an ordinary citizen you were to see these occupations as ways of working out your holy calling.

These, then, are questions of our human identity and human vocation: 'Who are we, and what is the ultimate meaning of our life? How do we find our vocation and identity in the situation in which we find ourselves?' The liturgical tradition of Christian spirituality, like many other traditions, has wrestled with these fundamental questions, believing that the challenge of aimlessness is not only a social and political challenge but a spiritual challenge as well. As we have seen, the liturgical tradition looks to a particular set of resources and uses a particular method for arriving at its answers; in every age, the tradition has been clear that the common prayer of the Church is the principal resource for people seeking to know who they are and how their particular life circumstances fit into the overall relationship with God.

THE SPIRIT OF THE LITURGY AND THE HUMAN SPIRIT

The clear and consistent witness of the liturgical tradition, from its beginnings in the New Testament period to the present day, has been that to enter into the 'spirit of the liturgy' is to enter into the arena of human spiritual transformation. As the Second Vatican Council's *Constitution on the Sacred Liturgy* says: 'Day by day the liturgy builds up those within the Church into the Lord's holy Temple, into a spiritual dwelling for God – an enterprise which will continue until Christ's full stature is achieved.'[2] As we have seen, representatives of the tradition differ in their understanding of exactly how this transformation happens. For some, the words, images and actions of the liturgy present a vision of the redeemed human person and human society; for others, corporate worship is the principal arena within which the Holy Spirit is present and active, forming and confirming human identity; for still others the infusion of God's self-giving love in and through the sacraments and other rites strengthens believers for participation in the creation of a humane and righteous future. In answer to the question 'What does the liturgy do?' liturgist Robert Taft takes account of all these things as he expresses the power of the liturgy in the shaping of our identity and vocation:

> It is in the liturgy that Christ, as the Church's head, acting through the Spirit in the Church's ministry, draws us into the saving paschal mystery. Baptized into the mystery of his death, we rise to new life in him, having 'put on Christ.'
>
> Henceforth, through his Spirit, he dwells in us, prays in us, proclaims to us the Word of his New Covenant and

seals it with his sacrifice on the cross, feeds us with his own body and blood, draws us to conversion and penance, glorifies the Father in us. In proclamation and preaching he explains to us his mystery; in rite and song he celebrates it with us; in sacramental grace he gives us the will and the strength to live it. When we leave the assembly to return to our mundane tasks, we have only to assimilate what we have experienced and realize this mystery in our lives; in a word, to become other Christs.[3]

Many in the tradition would also argue that part of the liturgy's task is to establish a Christian 'counter-culture' within which worshippers are able to reframe their identity and values. According to theologian Charles Davis, 'Our faith and worship are not part of the modern secular world in which we live, not part of its socially shared and conformed reality. As believers and worshippers we step outside the dominant secular culture as social deviants.'[4] If the liturgy establishes a 'counter-culture', it also provides strength for those who must endure the oppression and social isolation engendered by the dominant culture. As one politician observed about the relationship between worship and the nineteenth-century labour movement: 'The chapel gave them their first music, their first literature and philosophy to meet the harsh life and cruel impact of the crude materialistic age. Here men found the language and art to express antagonisms to grim conditions and injustice.'[5]

As we can see, in order for all these things to happen one must enter into a deep relationship with the Church's corporate worship. As Martin Thornton says in his description of the liturgical spirituality of William of St Thierry, 'we do not attend services of worship [in order] to "get to know what happens" or to "learn the service", or even to get into a good habit, but to *see* the faith externally as preparation to its contemplative absorption.'[6] In other words, if we are to find our true identity and our true vocation, we must become 'liturgical', down to the roots of our being. For all the representatives of the liturgical tradition of Christian spirituality, the common prayer of the Church invites us to participate in a new reality which transforms us into *persons*.

WHAT DOES IT MEAN TO BE A HUMAN BEING?

> Fragmented persons fashion fragmented worlds, and fragmented worlds produce fragmented persons.
>
> William R. Johnson[7]

> The modern ignorance is in people's assumptions that they can outsmart their own nature. It is arrogance that will believe nothing that cannot be proved, respect nothing it cannot understand, and value nothing it cannot sell.
>
> Wendell Berry[8]

In a world of conflicting and often manipulative messages about who and what we are, the answer to the question 'What does it mean to be a human being?' is not at all self-evident. Most within the liturgical tradition of Christian spirituality would say that if we are to find our way through this maze of messages and to get a clear sense of who and what we are, it will be by following the words and images of the Church's common prayer. As this takes place, the liturgical tradition has tended to highlight a number of themes, things that human beings learn about themselves in and through the liturgy.

First, we learn from the liturgy that our identity is grounded, not in our own attitude toward ourselves, but in God's attitude toward us. One exponent of the tradition says:

> In the light of the liturgy the Christian understands very well that creatures are not bad, but good, as works of God and traces of his infinite goodness, which has given them their being . . . The liturgy does not despise any creature, but brings them all into the church's universal worship of God through Jesus Christ, and for all of them she has appropriate blessings.[9]

The first thing the liturgy teaches about the human person, then, is that (in the words of the Second Vatican Council), all human beings are to be regarded as 'more precious for what they are than what they have'.[10] Whatever else we may be, we are uniquely precious in the sight of God.

But not only are we generally, as a species, precious to God, we are also precious to God as individual persons. This message is conveyed to us in a number of different ways in the liturgy. Orthodox liturgist Alexander Schmemann (1921–1997), using the Orthodox practice of naming a child on the eighth day after birth as an example, reflects on the deep relationship between Christian worship and human personality.

> The naming rite is the acknowledgment by the Church of the *uniqueness* of this particular child, of the divine gift of 'personality' . . . By referring it to God's Holy Name, the Church reveals each name to he holy, i.e., sanctified by the human name of Christ himself. In Christ, the name of each human being is shown to be the name of a child of God, created and destined for a *personal* relationship with God, a personal participation in God's eternal Kingdom.[11]

To be called 'holy' in the liturgy, even before we have 'accomplished' or 'earned' anything, establishes the baseline for our renewed sense of who we are as human beings.

Most representatives of the tradition would want to agree with Schmemann that in order to know what the human person is and can be we must look to Jesus Christ. And if we are to discover the true meaning of our own humanity, we must begin to conform ourselves to Christ's image. One of the earliest exponents of the tradition is the anonymous writer of the *Gospel According to Philip*. In a passage rich with liturgical imagery, he argues that in this process of human growth into the perfection of Christ, the sacraments of the Lord's Supper and baptism are the principal agents:

> The cup of prayer contains wine and contains water, being
> established as a representation of the blood over which
> thanksgiving is offered. And it is full of the Holy Spirit,
> and belongs entirely to the perfect human being. When-
> ever we drink it we take unto ourselves the perfect human
> being. The living water is a body. It befits us to put on the
> living human being; accordingly, when one is about to
> descend into the water, one strips naked in order to put
> that one on.[12]

To 'put on Christ' and to 'drink in Christ' are means by which
our transformation into the likeness of Christ takes place.

For others in the tradition, the beginnings of understanding
our true selves lie in the liturgy's establishment of new patterns of community, giving us a deeper sense of who we are in
relation with others; not only with other human beings, but
with God as well.

> In worship, we continue to learn our need so as to praise
> God for his justifying care. In worship, we also begin to
> perceive our gifts so as to do the work of the Gospel. In
> this sense, the justified Christian is, as the classical axiom
> states, both sinner and saint at the same time: sinner
> because what God has freely given has not been fully
> accepted; saint because the essential first step of salvation,
> God's justifying love, is already present.[13]

Saint and sinner, striving – if sometimes only haltingly –
toward the likeness of Christ, recipients from our creation of
the boundless love of God: the liturgical tradition is clear that
all these images of what it means to be a human person are
infused in us as we participate in the common prayer of the
Church.

Ordinary Christians often express this very same view,
although perhaps using more 'down-to-earth' ways of doing so.
Nine-year-old Mary is one example. Interviewed by American
psychiatrist Robert Coles, whose interest in the religious and
spiritual life of marginalised children has resulted in a series

of extraordinary records, Mary tells Coles about a particular worship service during which she had a clear sense of her vocation:

> When you're put here it's for a reason. The Lord wants you to do something. If you don't know what, then you've got to find out what... I was singing in Church last Sunday, and I thought that God must be enjoying us, because we were hitting all the notes just right!... I was thinking that maybe God put me here so I could sing like I did.[14]

All who stand within this tradition, then, whether great theologians or small children, have come to much the same conclusion. The common worship of the Church teaches us who we are by allowing us to *be* who we are; the liturgy teaches us our calling by inviting us to *exercise* that calling in the liturgical assembly.

WHAT DOES IT MEAN TO LIVE THE 'RISEN LIFE'?

> Our task is to make our lives (individual and corporate) *baptismal*, referred to the baptismal mystery as its source and nourishment.
>
> Alexander Schmemann[15]

Despite the liturgy's messages about the inherent worth of human persons, we each know that all is not as it should be. The reality of human sin, individual and corporate, presses upon us with every move we make. And the question that arises out of this situation is clear: How can this motley crew be God's instrument? For many within the tradition, the answer lies in the rites and practices of Christian initiation. Both those who baptise small children (paedo-baptists) and those who baptise only professing believers are agreed that the words and actions of baptism model our Christian vocation and give us the spiritual resources with which to carry out that vocation. The waters of baptism are linked thematically to the waters of the womb, bringing forth new life in Christ. As the East Syrian spiritual guide Jacob of Serugh (451–521) says:

> Christ came and opened up baptism on his Cross so that it might be, in the place of Eve, a 'mother of living beings' for the world; water and blood. For the fashioning of spiritual children, flowed forth and so baptism became the mother of life.[16]

Others look to images not from birth but from death, following Paul's imagery in Romans 6:6. We are new creatures because in baptism 'we know that our old self was crucified with him' (NRSV). For Martin Luther:

> It is indeed correct to say that Baptism is a washing away of sins, but the expression is too mild and weak to bring out the full significance of Baptism, which is rather a symbol of death and resurrection. For this reason I would have those who are baptized completely immersed in the water ... The sinner does not so much need to be washed as he needs to die, in order to be wholly renewed and made another creature and to be conformed to the death and resurrection of Christ with whom he dies and rises again through baptism.[17]

For most within the tradition, though, all of these images are blended together: new birth, crucifixion, purification. We can see this in one of the famous baptismal homilies of John Chrysostom:

> When you come to the sacred initiation, the eyes of the flesh see water; the eyes of faith see the Spirit. These eyes see the body being baptized; the eyes of the spirit see the old man being buried. The eyes of the flesh see the body being washed; the eyes of the spirit see the soul being cleansed. The eyes of the body see the body emerging from the water; the eyes of faith see the new man come forth brightly shining from that purification. Our bodily eyes

see the priest as, from above, he lays his right hand on the head and touches [the one being baptized]; our spiritual eyes see the great High Priest as He stretches forth his invisible hand to touch the head.[18]

For some within the tradition, our baptism is the place where we are given a new name. In some cases, especially in missionary situations, this is a literal renaming, signifying a radical change of identity. In his moving account of his work among the Masai in Africa, missionary Vincent Donovan tells of preparations for baptism in a small village, where one particularly devout convert is concerned with this question of finding a new name. He says to Donovan:

> Of all the stories you told us, one I like most. It attracts me, the story of the man who left everything and led his people from the worship of a tribal god in search of the unknown High God. If you permit me, I would like to be called Abraham.[19]

In this case, the change of name has become symbolic of a change of life and a change of vocation, from the worship of a 'tribal god' to the worship of 'High God' who had become known to him. To be given this new name is not only symbolic of a new relationship with God, but it is symbolic of being 'relocated' into a new spiritual geography:

> In our baptism, wherein we gave up our names to Christ, we became denizens and freemen of heaven. All the difference between them [the saints] and us is only this, that we are abroad, and they are at home; we on this, and they on the other side of Jordan; we in the acquest and they in possession of the heavenly Canaan.[20]

Whether being given a 'new name' is literal or symbolic, the conviction is the same throughout the tradition: in baptism we are given a new identity. At our baptism, remarks one contemporary Lutheran liturgist,

Our identity for all the days of our life is set! We are

children of God, priests of the King, disciples of Christ, a servant people, a holy nation, a communion of saints, the followers of the Way, proclaimers of the wonderful deeds of God. Jesus' story becomes our story.[21]

It is not only in the giving of a new name, however, that the rites of Christian initiation signify this new identity. It was ancient practice to clothe the newly baptised in white garments, which would be worn for the entire week after baptism (a time called, appropriately, the 'Week of White Garments'). Cyril of Jerusalem, in a sermon preached during that week to those who had been baptised at Easter, refers to these garments as a symbol of Christian identity:

> Now that you have put off your old garments, and have put on those which are spiritually pure, you must be clad in white always. I do not, of course, mean literally that your clothes must always be white, but that you must be clad in those truly white and shining spiritual garments, so that you may say with the blessed Isaiah: 'Let my soul rejoice in the Lord, for he has dressed me in the garment of salvation, and with robes of gladness he has clothed me.'[22]

And yet whatever this 'new' identity is, it is somehow also rooted in the 'old' identity. Speaking of the rite of confirmation, Orthodox theologian Alexander Schmemann says:

> My confirmation is the confirmation of *myself*, to be what God wants me to be, what he has loved in me from all eternity. It is the gift of vocation . . . This is the 'wind,' the *ruah* of God entering our life, embracing it with fire and love, making us available for divine action, filling everything with joy and hope.[23]

The new baptismal identity, then, is built upon the identity which God planted within us at our creation. In the rites of Christian initiation, that identity is affirmed and God's promise to keep on restoring us in light of that identity is asserted.

Baptism is also the place in which we affirm our willingness to co-operate with these promises. In a famous passage from his treatise on baptism, the third-century theologian Tertullian makes this point in a word-play upon the traditional image of Christ as the 'fish' (which is taken from the ancient Greek monogram for Christ – Jesus [*I*esus] Christ [*CH*ristos] Son of God [*THeos*] Saviour [*Soter*] = 'ICHTHUS' which is the Greek word for 'fish'). Tertullian says, 'But we, being little fishes, as Jesus Christ is our Great Fish, begin our life in the water, and only while we abide in the water are we safe and sound.' In commenting on this passage, contemporary sacramental theologian Regis Duffy says that baptism then becomes an object of proclamation which 'repeatedly calls Christians to the obedience into which they have been taken in Baptism ... To "remain in the water with Jesus" is, in effect, to live out such obedience at each stage of our lives.'[24]

And so, in this new baptismal identity we are both, in Paul's words, 'in the world but not of it'. In our baptism we are drawn into the ministry of Christ which includes Christ's priesthood, and therefore have a responsibility for bearing the burdens of a hurt and broken world.

> We are not 'nice' Christians come apart from the ugly world. If we do not stand precisely as representatives of the world, as indeed the world itself, if we do not bear the whole burden of THIS day, our 'poetry' may still be pious, but not Christian.[25]

Although other aspects of the liturgy confirm and reinforce our baptismal identity, it is within the various aspects of the rites of Christian initiation that we see clearly how this person, this 'motley crew', can indeed be God's instrument. By being immersed not only in the waters of baptism, but also by being immersed in the words and images of the rites, we discover the multifaceted human identity which God has created and redeemed.

THE LITURGICAL SPIRITUALITY OF EMBODIMENT

It is not easy to think clearly about the meaning of the body in the formation of our human identity and vocation in the world in which we live. Day in and day out we are bombarded with messages about our human bodies; we are told (primarily by those who wish to sell us their products) that the proper shape, smell, fitness, strength of our bodies are vitally important to who and what we are. The liturgical tradition of Christian spirituality also believes our human bodies are important to our human identity and vocation. But the messages we get from the liturgy about the importance of our bodies are markedly different from the messages sent by the world in which we live.

The tradition certainly recognises the human potential for using the body in ways that are ultimately destructive to our relationship with God and with others. In the liturgy, however, we begin the process of allowing our bodies to be fed on 'pure food', which will effect in us a change, from a body marked by corruption to a body marked by resurrection life. As one early exponent of the tradition puts it, in the liturgy

> the Lord supplies ... the foods most appropriate for us. He proffers his flesh and pours out his blood and nothing is lacking to the children for their good. O paradoxical mystery! He commands us to put off the old fleshly corruption, and the old nourishment as well, to partake of another, new way of life, that of Christ, to receive him, if possible, and store him up in ourselves, to put the Savior in our hearts, in order to destroy the passions of the flesh.[26]

As we have already seen, contemporary exponents of the tradition express this same understanding by quoting the words of Feuerbach, 'You are what you eat'. If you 'partake' of the liturgical life of the Church, then you are gradually transformed by its words, images and gestures. In both Eucharist and Baptism, then, our bodies are 're-created' so that they might become vehicles for righteousness, prepared for a lively response to the will of God. In this way they contribute to the formation, rather than the deformation, of our human identity.

This linking between our bodies and our identity is forged in a number of ways in the liturgy. First, our bodies are essential to the act of remembering, which is seen to lie at the very heart of our self-identity. Christians have always believed that (in the words that are inscribed in the Holocaust Museum in Jerusalem), 'To remember is the beginning of redemption'. But the liturgical tradition wants to argue that we remember not only with our minds but with our bodies. Historian Paul Connerton observes that the most deeply held values and priorities within communities are often 'embodied' rather than simply placed in texts or 'committed to memory'. 'How well the past can be kept in mind is determined by a habitual memory sedimented in the body.'[27] This is a more 'holistic' approach to memory than we are accustomed to. The tradition is clear that such things as kneeling, washing, raising our hands in praise, and processing have more than just 'ceremonial' value. It is in and through these actions of our bodies that the memory of our redemption is kept alive.

In addition, such common bodily functions as eating, drinking and washing become in the liturgy means by which the relationship with God and other human beings is nourished. Indian theologian Raimundo Panikkar describes the process by which this takes place:

> People eat. It is the eating that has to be transformed by the sacramental presence and thus the Eucharist had to regain its symbolism of being a meal. People dance and amuse themselves. Christian worship has here again to recover its aspect of celebration and festivity. People are born, come of age, get married, adopt a profession, and die. The sacraments have to sanctify and consecrate these most universal and elemental human acts. The sacraments of Initiation, Maturity, Marriage, etc., must not be simply ceremonies and traditional ritualisms, but have a real bearing and meaning for these important moments

of human existence; in a word, they must really shape them . . . Worship has to permeate human life once again and render it more meaningful, enhancing the significance of those acts and also giving the necessary strength (grace) for one to live up to such a human calling.[28]

The liturgy also teaches us about the proper place of the body in human relationships of all kinds. 'Ritual acts of touching, such as footwashing and exchanging signs of peace in worship, offer us opportunities to learn to touch one another in peace and love.'[29] This may be singularly important in an age in which exploitative human touching is so common. We learn from the liturgy, and especially from the way the liturgy invites our human bodies to act, how we are to be together as embodied beings in the world.

In delightfully impressionistic language, Welsh poet and artist David Jones accurately describes the value of the human body within the liturgical tradition of Christian spirituality: 'Without body: without sacrament. Angels only: no sacrament. Beasts only: no sacrament. Man sacrament at every turn and all levels of the "profane" and "sacred" in the trivial and in the profound, no escape from sacrament.'[30] He is, of course, using the term 'sacrament' in both its wide and narrow sense. There can be no tangible manifestation of the presence and love of God without bodies. Moreover, for the liturgical tradition of spirituality, there an be no tangible manifestation of the presence and love of God without *our* bodies.

THE SPIRITUAL MEANING OF LIFE COMMITMENTS

Our identities are not only linked to the reality of our human bodies, but also to the reality of our deepest human relationships. Life commitments, especially Christian marriage, have always been seen to have particular value in the spiritual life, as true vocational paths; and the liturgical celebration of these events has, by various means, always made this point. On the other hand, it is hard to underestimate the degree to which intimate human relationships can be distorted, and harder to underestimate the untold human misery caused of this distortion. The liturgical tradition is clear that if a true sense of the meaning of these life commitments is to be gained and incorporated within our sense of ourselves and our calling, then we must avail ourselves of the spirit of the liturgy.

Marriage, of course, is not unique to Christianity. But as we saw with the other ordinary human actions like eating, drinking, and washing, it can be transformed into a vehicle for living more deeply the relationship with God. Marriage as a Christian vocation begins with the partners 'accepting each other as a gift of God, by mutual appreciation, kindness, patience and healing forgiveness'.[31] It continues by seeing the married couple as called to participate in the wider mission of God which, in the words of one contemporary marriage rite, requires the couple to live in such a way 'that those to whom love is a stranger may find in them generous friends'.

> [The true meaning of the sacrament of matrimony] is not that it merely gives a 'religious sanction' to marriage and family life, reinforces with supernatural grace the natural family virtues. Its meaning is that by taking the 'natural' marriage into the 'great Mystery of Christ and the Church,' the sacrament of matrimony gives marriage a new meaning, transforms, in fact, not only marriage as such, but all human love.[32]

In and through the liturgy, human love becomes a sign of the love of God; the love of two ordinary people becomes a sacrament of God's fidelity, God's mercy, and God's perpetual promise to forgive.

In this way, the community formed by the marriage between two people becomes a 'Church in microcosm', a primary cell of Christian spirituality. As an Orthodox representative of the tradition says, looking at his own tradition of 'crowning' the bride and groom in the wedding rite:

> This is what the marriage crowns express: that here is

the beginning of a small kingdom, which *can* be something like the true Kingdom. The chance will be lost, perhaps even in one night; but at this moment it is still an open possibility. Yet even when it had been lost, and lost again a thousand times, still if two people stay together, they are in a real sense king and queen to each other. And after forty odd years, Adam can still turn and see Eve standing beside him, in a unity with himself which in some small way at least proclaims the love of God's Kingdom.[33]

The marriage becomes, then, not only a Church in microcosm, but also a recapitulation of Eden, a new chance for a godly relationship between man and woman.

THE PLACE OF WORK IN THE RELATIONSHIP WITH GOD

Like other aspects of our identity and vocation, human work presents us with very real difficulties in the contemporary world. Unemployment, underemployment, exploitation, over-work, the increasing disparity in earnings between rich and poor, between First and Third World labourers: all of these things colour our approach to and attitude toward work. 'In a madly competitive world,' one contemporary theologian observes, 'the question of power touches our most sensitive spot. Incompetence causes us more shame than sin. Success is the only credential we know.'[34] Whether we are working or unemployed, underemployed or pensioned, both the idea and practice of work have become burdensome and enslaving, rather than creative and liberating. One observer of the con-temporary world of work asks: 'Is there time to make a new paradigm of work part of our thinking in the future, so that the cross of work becomes a sign of hope?'[35] The liturgical tradition is clear that a renewal of the meaning of work is both possible and necessary, that work can be incorporated creatively into the spiritual life, and that this process will

begin with participation in patterns of life exemplified by corporate worship.

It must be said that the liturgical tradition has not ignored
the fact that the world of work and its attendant distractions
can hinder the liturgy's work of human transformation. The
fourteenth-century mystic Walter Hilton, among the most
practical exponents of the liturgical tradition, warns of the
difficulties which arise when the working life intrudes on
the life of corporate prayer: 'The prayer of other men that are
busied in active works is made of two words. For they oft times
form in their hearts one word through thinking of worldly
business, and sound in their mouth another word of the psalm
sung or said.'[36]

But all is not lost, even for the distracted worker; it is the
inclination of the heart which is the final determiner of
the potency of our prayer. Hilton concludes by saying, 'nevertheless if their intent be true, yet it is their prayer good and
needful, though it lack savor and sweetness'. Because the liturgical tradition has never made the sharp dichotomy between
'secular' and 'sacred' concerns, it is a natural starting-point for
a new vision of the place of work in quest for God and godliness.

As a part of this process, many contemporary representatives of the liturgical tradition invite us to return to the
liturgical spirituality embedded in the Jewish practice of
Sabbath-keeping to renew and re-envision human labour. The
Jewish Sabbath has always been about liberation, recalling
the liberation from slavery in Egypt and ritualised in the
Passover seder. As one proponent of Christian Sabbath-
keeping says:

> Authentic sabbath time implies *freedom* and invites fresh
> eyes and fresh breath with which to see and be in the
> world. We are freed from the often narrow sight and limits
> of workaday living. Life can be seen from the mountaintop
> and saved from submission to such temptations as the
> clouded valleys of fatalism, compulsive drudgery, rigid
> roles and relationships, and divisions and controls that

warp and paralyze our responsiveness to the Spirit's presence.[37]

The Sabbath has also been about creation, and about God's willingness to rest and to declare that all creation is good. To celebrate the Sabbath, then, is to recognise that the creativity of our work is rooted in and dependent upon the wider creativity of God.

Others in the tradition wish to say that any hope for a renewal of the idea of work will be found in the practice of liturgical feasting. To celebrate a 'feast', the tradition argues, is to move into a new mode of being human. The liturgist Lluis Duch writes:

> Feasts are characterized by human encounters devoted not to greater work effort, but to feeling, intuiting the unity, fullness and beauty of reality, beyond the apparent chaos and distortion of the everyday. So the authentic feast exists on a plane beyond dogma and ethics, in the sphere of *gratuitousness* and *fullness of meaning*. Going beyond the language of prescription, the 'unsayable' produces its Epiphany.[38]

The key to the transformation of work, then, lies in our ability to learn to celebrate, to become 'homo festivus', a festival being. For the person who is a true participant in the feast, everything becomes fully alive, and he or she is attentive and responsive to the movement of the Spirit.

As the primary 'feast' of the Christian liturgical life, the Eucharist teaches us that all things come to us as a gift; that we do not create from nothing, that even our work is a working with what has first been given us:

> No one has been 'worthy' to receive communion, no one has been *prepared* for it. At this point all merits, all righteousness, all devotions disappear and dissolve. Life comes again to us *as gift*, a free and divine gift . . . Adam is again introduced into Paradise, taken out of nothingness, and crowned king of creation. Everything is free,

nothing is due, and yet all is given. And, therefore, the greatest humility and obedience is to accept the gift, to say 'yes' – in joy and gratitude. There is nothing we can *do*, yet we become all that God wanted us to be from eternity, when we are *eucharistic*.[39]

In the Lord's Supper, the work of human hands, bread baked and wine made, vessels crafted and textiles woven, the money in the offering plate, all become transparent to the redemptive love of God. This allows us to see our work for what it is, a true participation in the life and mission of God.

In this, the liturgical tradition is clear and consistent: whatever you do must be set within the wider mission of God which is the restoration and redemption of all things. Søren Kierkegaard's words capture the spirit of the liturgical tradition when he enquires:

'What is your occupation in life?' We do not ask inquisitively about whether it is great or mean, whether you are a king or only a labourer. [We do] not ask, after the fashion of business, whether you earn a great deal of money or are building up a great prestige for yourself. The crowd inquires and talks of these things. But whether your occupation is great or mean, is it of such a kind that you dare to think of it with the responsibility of eternity?[40]

To set human work within the overall work of God, creative, transformative, redemptive, will allow both for its liberation and its direction toward its true goal. In addition, to allow the liturgy to provide for us new models for the understanding of work will result in a new kind of 'self':

Imagine a self, no longer the self of consumer advertising, no longer a self caught in endless efforts of self-security, but a self rooted in the inscrutable miracle of God's love, a self no longer consigned to the rat race, but one oriented to full communion with God – which is true destiny and rightful home. Imagine such a self present regularly to the scripting of the sermon, present regularly to the sacraments of generosity.[41]

To be present to the various liturgical images and gestures is to allow the liturgy not only to set a new trajectory for work, but for the whole human person, a trajectory which takes account all of the manifestations and difficulties of the world of work and allows us to integrate work into the spiritual life in a way that is both creative and redemptive.

A 'UNIVERSE IN MINIATURE'

The liturgical tradition has generally not been content to define the human person and the human vocation solely in terms of the mission of God on earth, as important as that may be. It also wishes to set human identity and vocation within the vocation of the whole created order to praise and glorify God. In the liturgy, as we blend our voices with Christians past and present we also insert ourselves into the deepest reality of the universe. As Quaker theologian Thomas Kelly puts it:

> Our prayers are mingled with a vaster Word, a Word that at one time was made flesh. We pray, and yet it is not we who pray, but a Greater who prays in us ... All we can say is 'Prayer is taking place, and I am given to be in the orbit.' In holy hush we bow in Eternity, and know the Divine Concern tenderly enwrapping us and all things in his persuading love.[42]

Rather than resulting in a diminution of our individuality as human beings, this establishes within us our true and eternal identity. Kelly continues: 'Here the autonomy of the inner life becomes complete, and we are joyfully *prayed through* by a Seeking Life that flows through us into the world of men.'[43]

Within the liturgical tradition, the common prayer of the Christian community becomes a means by which we 'attune ourselves' to this wider vocation. The third-century apologist

Clement of Alexandria actually speaks of us as 'God's instruments', instruments which are tuned to a 'new song', and through the liturgy:

> Behold the power of this new song! It has changed stones into people, to life again, just by hearing this song. Yes, this song, has arranged the universe in harmonious order ... so that the whole world might become a melody ... making us humans – composed of body and spirit – a universe in miniature.[44]

Almost universally among the early exponents of the tradition we find this notion that participation in the liturgy on earth inserts the worshipper into the liturgy which is going on eternally before the throne of God. But in a commentary on the opening dialogue of the Great Thanksgiving over the eucharistic elements of bread and wine ('Lift up your hearts! We have them with the Lord'), John Chrysostom goes even further. In the dialogue, worshippers declare their hearts to be in heaven praising God; 'But,' says Chrysostom, 'what do I care about heaven, when I myself have become heaven?' The liturgy so infuses believers with the grace of God that everything that is meant by the word 'heaven' can now be used in describing worshippers themselves.

Other elements of the liturgy also 'tune us' to the song of the heavenly hosts. In a sermon to those who have been baptised at Easter, Cyril of Jerusalem explains to the neophytes the meaning of the ancient hymn called the *sanctus* which is sung as a part of the eucharistic liturgy.[45]

> After that we call to mind the heavens, the earth and the seam the sun and moon, the stars, the whole rational and irrational creation, both visible and invisible. Angels and archangels, virtues, dominions, principalities and powers, thrones, and the many-faced cherubim ... We call to mind also the seraphim, whom Isaiah, in the Holy Spirit, saw encircling the throne of God, 'with two wings veiling their faces, while flying with two saying 'Holy, holy, holy, Lord

of Hosts.' (Is 6:23) *We recite this doxology which comes to us from the Seraphim that we may be sharers of the hymnody of the heavenly hosts.*[46]

In every age, representatives of the liturgical tradition link the capacity of the liturgy to 'tune our lives to the rhythms of the universe' directly to the practice of liturgical singing. Over and over again, from Augustine's fourth-century dictum 'Whoever sings prays twice' to Huub Oosterhuis' twentieth-century observation that 'Singing is born at times when there is no other possible way for people to express themselves', we hear the tradition claiming that music is both the proper language of the human soul, and also a language which has a particular power within the divine–human relationship.

> The act of singing together is deeply and indelibly human. When we sing, words are given greater range and power than when we speak. Something is shared in singing that goes beyond the words alone. Among Christians, this something has taken shape over many centuries in a practice that expresses our deepest yearning and dearest joy: the practice of singing our lives.[47]

Indeed, deep in the tradition is embedded the image that the whole Christian life can be summed up in a liturgical-musical analogy: in responding to the invitation of faith, 'We become singers of a new song.' 'We are Easter people and "alleluia" is our song.'[48]

To join in the liturgy, then, is to sing the hymn of the universe, the hymn of the celestial hierarchy, the hymn of the Church, the hymn of the human soul. In this way corporate worship has the capacity to deepen and enlarge our idea of what it means to be a human being. In his treatise on the nature and purpose of the Church, Deitrich Bonhoeffer sings his own hymn to the power of the liturgy:

> 'Sing unto the Lord a new song,' the Psalter enjoins us again and again. It is the Christ-hymn, new every morning, that the family fellowship strikes up at the

beginning of the day, the hymn that is sung by the whole Church of God on earth and in heaven to which we are summoned to join. God has prepared for himself one great song of praise throughout eternity, and those who enter the community of God join in this song . . . In the morning of every day the Church on earth lifts up this song and in the evening it closes the day with this hymn. It is the Triune God and His works that are extolled.[49]

But the tradition is also clear that while we are alive we are always situated between two worlds. And despite the capacity of the liturgy to give us a vision of our place within the wider vocation of the created universe, we will always be striving to fulfil that vocation. Bonhoeffer continues with his analogy of song as a metaphor for the Christian life: 'This song has a different ring on earth from what it is in heaven. On earth it is the song of those who believe, in heaven the song of those who see.'

Which brings the liturgical tradition full-circle, back to the question of our earthly human vocation, our identity, not as angels but as human beings who participate in the mission of God. To participate in the liturgy is to participate in the glorification of God. And to participate in the glorification of God has certain very real consequences for all of our relationships. As one twentieth-century representative of the liturgical tradition of Christian spirituality says:

The worship of God is primarily concerned with giving God the glory – and to give God the glory is to make us what we are intended to be: [God's] beloved children. When that understanding is seen as central, when it is at the heart of life, and of things, then it will follow, as the night the day, that the Christian will want to bring everything else into conformity with that ennobling vision.[50]

3. ESTABLISHING COMMUNITY

> Our prayer is public and common; and when we pray, we
> pray not for one, but for the whole people, because the
> whole people are one.
>
> Cyprian of Carthage

If the liturgy is the basis for discovering what it means to be
a human person for the liturgical tradition of spirituality, it is
also the basis for discovering what it means to be a community
of persons. Community formation is not easy. It takes many
competencies that the workaday world rarely teaches or
rewards: humility, co-operation, forgiveness, imagination,
interdependence, vulnerability. Throughout the liturgical tradition there is the deep conviction that not only does the liturgy
help us to develop these traits necessary for the formation of
true human community, but is also, in the relationships it
fosters and models, a sign to the world of how that community
is intended by God to look and behave.

THE IMPORTANCE OF THE LITURGICAL COMMUNITY

The witness of the liturgical tradition, from the first century
onwards, is that to be a Christian is to gather with other
Christians to worship God, and that the spirituality of the
liturgy is activated wherever 'two or three are gathered' in
Christ's name. Indeed, the ancient writers were unequivocal
that not only are individuals spiritually disabled by not being
present for public worship, but that the Church as a whole is

also weakened. One fourth-century document which sets out the rules for ordering church life advises church leaders:

> Teach the people by precepts and exhortations to attend the assembly without fail: let them always be present, let them never diminish the Church by their absence, and let them never deprive the Body of Christ of one of its members. Each should take as for himself, not for others, the words of Christ: 'He who does not gather with me scatters' (Mt 12: 30; Luke 11: 23). Since you are the members of Christ, you must not be scattered outside the Church by neglecting to come together.[1]

In every age, the liturgical tradition repeats this admonition in one way or another. Monk and theologian Maximus the Confessor (580–662), one of the most authoritative of the tradition's representatives, says that the power of the liturgy is activated when the Church gathers because the angels in heaven 'take note each time people enter and present themselves to God, and make supplication for them'.[2] In addition, he continues, because the Holy Spirit is particularly present for the celebration of the liturgy, it is imperative that believers gather together in order to avail themselves of the Spirit's power which 'transforms and changes each person who is found there and in fact remolds him in proportion to what is more divine in him'.[3]

The tradition also describes ways in which the various individual elements of the liturgy reinforce this idea that it is a spiritual necessity for Christians to come together as a worshipping community. In his 'Homily on Matthew', Bishop John Chrysostom reflects on the essential actions of the Eucharist as the model for Christian solidarity:

> There are many things indeed which bring us together. One table is set for all, one Father begot us, we are all born of the same birth pangs, the same drink has been given to all, or, rather, not only the same drink, but even to drink from one cup. For our Father, wishing to bring

us to familial affection, has devised this also, that we should drink from one cup, a thing which belongs to intimate love.[4]

This image of a shared table implicating us in a shared life, and indeed a shared life of a particular quality, is expanded upon as Chrysostom continues:

> We have shared a spiritual table, let us also share spiritual love. For if robbers, sharing a meal, forget their usual behavior, what excuse will we have, who are continually sharing the Lord's body and do not even imitate their gentleness? And yet to many, not only one table, but even to be of one city has been sufficient basis for friendship; but we, when we have the same city, and the same house and table, and Way, and Door, and Root, and Life and Teacher, and Judge and Creator and to whom all things are in common – what forgiveness can be deserved if we are divided from one another?[5]

Indeed, it is not only that the liturgy builds us into a community, but also that the quality of our relationships within that community 'build' the liturgy. The Creed in the Byzantine Liturgy, for example, is introduced with the words, 'Let us love one another, that with one mind we may confess Father, Son and Holy Spirit.' If our prayer is to reach its full spiritual potency, our love for one another within the Christian community must be genuine.

Within the liturgical assembly, then, union with one another is both achieved and made visible as the prayers of individuals are gathered together. In addition, a common sense of God's *purpose* for the community is engendered. A Quaker witness to the tradition puts it this way:

> The living power of the meeting for worship [arises through] a united communion in the presence of God wherein each one overpasses the bounds of his individual self and knows a union of spirit with spirit, bringing him into a larger life than that which is known in spiritual

separateness ... We cannot come to a true understanding of life's purposes apart from knowledge of one another in the deepest place of our being ... Out of such fellowship there will arise a sense of common purpose in life and the ... consciousness that in varied fashion all are ministering in the service of God.[6]

In the liturgy, then, we are invited into a deep union with one another, which is achieved through a deep union with the God who is the ultimate source of our unity. In all of these examples from the tradition it is clear, however, that the community that is formed and manifested in the liturgy is neither accidental nor arbitrary. It is a community which has particular qualities which are rooted in the sense of who God is and how God acts.

THE REALITY OF COMMUNITY IN CHRIST

The primary 'community-forming' action is the redemption of humankind in Jesus Christ, which is the ground of any and all liturgical celebration. Christ's prayer 'that they all may be one' (John 17:23) is to be expressed in both liturgy and life, as those who are intimately related to Christ in baptism and in the celebration of the Lord's Supper live out the reality of their relationship with all others who are 'in Christ'. The striking metaphor that Paul uses for this reality is a human body: in Christ we are the members of 'one body' (1 Corinthians 10:17), like the hands, feet, eyes, ears of a physical body (1 Corinthians 12). Others in the tradition carry this metaphor further. Augustine of Hippo in a moving sermon from the beginning of the fifth century, expounds on Paul's linking of the formation of 'one body in Christ' to the sharing in the 'one bread' of the Lord's Supper:

'One bread,' [the Apostle] said. No matter how many loaves were placed before him then, there was only one bread. No matter how many loaves are placed on the altar of Christ throughout the world, it is but one bread ... This

bread is the Body of Christ, to which the Apostle refers
when he addresses the Church: 'Now you are the Body of
Christ and its members.' What you receive, you yourselves
are, and by the grace by which you have been redeemed,
you show agreement when you respond 'Amen'. What you
see here is the sacrament of unity.[7]

If 'we are what we eat' in the Supper, then the substances of
bread and wine themselves become a symbol of what must
happen to us, how we are to be related to one another. In the
words of the *Didache*, one of the most ancient of extant church
documents, 'As this piece of bread was once scattered grain
over the hillsides and was then brought together and made
one, so let your Church be brought together from the ends of
the earth.'[8]

For Martin Luther, our fellowship is not only symbolised but
also deepened each time we participate in the Eucharist, and
indeed God has provided the sacramental signs precisely so
that we might become a true community. For Luther, God
appointed the form of the Supper to 'stimulate and motivate
us to this fellowship'. Expanding upon the ancient words of
the *Didache*, he says:

> For just as the bread is made out of many grains ground
> and mixed together, and out of the bodies of many grains
> there comes the body of one bread, in which each grain
> loses its form and body and takes upon itself the common
> body of the bread; and just as the drops of wine, in losing
> their own form become the body of the common wine and
> drink – so it is and should be with us, if we use this
> sacrament properly ... In this way we are changed into
> one another and are made into a community of love.[9]

To be 'changed into one another' in and through participation
in the Supper is to partake of the deep sense of community
which the liturgical tradition believes necessary to any authentic Christianity, any authentic spirituality.

Some within the tradition wish to describe this unity with

one another as being primarily a deep, spiritual communion. Using the ancient liturgical action of the sharing of the 'kiss of peace' as an allegory for the reality of spiritual fellowship, John Chrysostom exhorts his hearers:

> Let us always be mindful ... of the holy kisses and the awe-inspiring embrace which we give one another. For this joins our minds, and causes us all to become one body, for, in fact, we all share one Body. Let us blend ourselves into one body, not mingling bodies with one another, but joining our souls to one another with the bond of love.[10]

For most within the tradition, however, this union that is engendered by sharing in common prayer is more than simply a spiritual kinship (in the narrow sense of the word). It also implicates us in the reality of one another's lives, to be in relationships of mutual care and compassion. One Anglican hymn-writer (who was incidentally also Prime Minister of Great Britain) describes this kind of relationship as he reflects upon the connection between sharing one food in the Lord's Supper and sharing in the lives of others:

> We, who with one blest Food are fed,
> Into one body may we grow,
> And one pure life from thee, the Head,
> Informing all the members flow;
> One pulse be felt in every vein,
> One law of pleasure and of pain.[11]

In the community which the liturgy envisions, then, we share all things in Christ: pleasure and pain, joy and sorrow. We build one another up and the absence of even one person from the assembly for worship is a diminishment of the whole Church: thus, as Martin Luther puts it, 'love engenders love in return and mutual love unites'.[12] Indeed, the Christian community described in Acts took the implications of this liturgical spirituality of community to its logical conclusion, proposing a quite radical sharing of economic resources. Those who are 'one in Christ' 'hold all things in common' (Acts 2:44), and this radical solidarity is mirrored in the words and actions of the liturgy.

THE MODELLING OF TRUE COMMUNITY

For many in this tradition, the Christian congregation itself – the liturgical assembly gathered before God in the name of Jesus Christ – is the sign of the beginnings of the new world that God is always in the process of creating. By standing before God, open to the will of God, ready and listening for the voice of God, the Christian congregation becomes a 'sacrament', a visible presence, of the saving will of God in the world. Contemporary Roman Catholic theologian Juan Segundo argues:

> In order to make its own specific and divine contribution to universal salvation, the visible Church qua community must be a sign, a sign of that universal salvific plan, of the recapitulation for which the whole universe is waiting, of a message that God sends through his church in order to contribute toward solutions of [our] historical problems that are truly human.[13]

In order to be a sacramental sign, however, the liturgical assembly must actually *look* like that reality of which it is the sign: it must be ordered and configured in such a way that it is evident to all who see it that the accomplishment of that 'universal salvific plan' has begun.

With this in mind, many representatives of the liturgical tradition of Christian spirituality invite us to look to the liturgy as an environment within which we might learn the shape of the true human community and to rehearse our roles as members of this community. 'The liturgical assembly', says another contemporary Roman Catholic, is 'neither a classroom nor a political rally. It is more like a rehearsal room where actions must be repeated over and over until they are thoroughly assimilated and perfected – until, that is, the actors have totally identified with the part assigned to them.'[14] In other words, it is within the liturgical assembly, where gifts are shared equally, service offered liberally, voices raised freely and joyfully, that we begin to model godly human relationships, renewed and restored in the light of the resurrection.

What might this restored human community actually look like? On the surface it would seem that those within this tradition have widely different answers for this question, coming as they do from communities which organise themselves in various different ways. But at the heart of the spiritual vision of the liturgical tradition is a single principle of community organisation, which is summed up by one contemporary representative of the tradition: 'The hearty gestures and symbols of the liturgy ... forever revolutionize our relations with others.'[15] The liturgical assembly is not just any ordinary social structure, organised around our common interests or even our common humanity, but rather is rooted in a 'common humanity as assumed and redeemed by the love and obedience of Jesus, and raised to a new level by the Spirit of Jesus at work in the world'.[16] The liturgical tradition is clear that the assembly for worship is called to be the paradigm of a community within which God's justice, peace and loving-kindness prevail.

This makes our love for one another 'not just a vague ethical imperative, but an expression of the new life to which they have, by no merits of their own, been reborn and which is essentially communal'. 'It is in the actual historical community into which they have been incorporated that the new life is to be worked out and brought to full realization in the perfected personhood of each of the children of God.'[17] In this process, the liturgy is the key.

> The liturgical assembly, at least in its ideal form, offers a model of such interaction. It is not a community of equals, but a community of God-given and complementary charisms, gifts that cannot be identified *a priori* by the categories of the secular community – age, sex, race – but are distributed by God indiscriminately among all for the

sole purpose of building up the community in perfect justice.[18]

We already see clear indications of this approach in Paul's deep concern for the worship life of the Corinthian Church, and particularly in his insistence that the social dichotomies which prevail in the world-at-large are not carried into the liturgical assembly (1 Corinthians 11:23ff). And it is carried further by an ancient treatise on church administration which insists that if a poor person comes into church, a place is to be found for her, 'even if you, O Bishop, have to sit on the ground!'[19]

A COMMUNITY OF SHARED GIFTS

> Liturgy is not something separate from the Church, but is simply the Church caught in the act of being most overtly itself as it stands faithfully in the presence of the One who is both object and source of that faith.
>
> Aidan Kavanagh[20]

For the liturgical tradition, the key to the formation of such a community lies in the way participation in the liturgy is achieved. The community which is mirrored in and established by the liturgy is a community of shared gifts; it is a community in which whatever we have – personal attributes, skills, goods, energy, faith – are shared within the community for, in Paul's words, the 'building up of the Body of Christ' (Ephesians 4:12). While this is the overall organising principle of the Christian community, according to the liturgical tradition it is the liturgy itself which is the arena within which these gifts are called forth, manifested and used. This sharing of human gifts is not simply a practical necessity or a useful and effective political design, but rather a practice which has a deep theological grounding, accurately reflecting God's sharing of God's gifts with us:

There is no grace or empowerment in being merely recipients of special favors in a grand action of divine charity. We receive more honor than that in being called to offer ourselves as partners in God's plan and process of renewal in the world. The wonder and grace of it all is that God wishes to carry out God's creative and saving work, not without us, but with us! And therein is the meaning and purpose of life as given by God.[21]

In the liturgy, then, our whole relationship with God is being modelled as our various gifts are called forth for the sake of the building up of the community and wider mission of God in and for the world.

This is not to say that there is no differentiation of roles within the liturgical assembly. In most concrete instances (with the possible exception of the Quaker Meeting) roles are quite clearly defined. But however they are defined, designated and recognised, roles within the Christian community are never simply pragmatic or arbitrary; rather, they are to be taken on after prayerful discernment of the spiritual gifts that have been given by God. While all of these roles within the assembly are important, some carry with them special responsibility for the health and well-being of the whole community, and some persons are set apart through ordination for these kinds of ministries. But even in these cases, while there may be community without office, there is never office without community. In fact, as Augustine recognises in words to the Church at Hippo when he was elected its bishop, the spiritual pitfalls of office are only avoided in community: 'When I am frightened by what I am for you, then I am consoled by what I am with you. For you I am a bishop; with you I am a Christian. The first is an office, the second a grace; the first a danger, the second salvation.'[22]

For the liturgical tradition, however, any and all ministries within the community are derived from the commissioning for ministry which all Christians receive in their baptism.

[I]n baptism by water and the Holy Spirit ... one is anointed with as full a sacerdotality as the Church possesses in and by the Anointed One himself. Ordination cannot make one more priestly than the Church, and without baptism, ordination cannot make one a priest at all. Becoming a Christian and becoming a sacerdotal being are not merely correlative processes, they are one and the same.[23]

Priesthood, then, is first and always a quality of the Church, and in order to exercise that priesthood in and for the world various roles and ministries are established. These roles and ministries are never for the sake of maximising the designated individual's spiritual growth and relationship with God (although this may indeed be a result), but always for the sake of the building up of the priestly vocation of the whole community, which is to enable the world to see the presence of the reign of God in its midst.

All of this implies that roles in the Christian community are going to be set by a different set of categories and priorities than the world has established. And it is the liturgy that sets these priorities forth in visible form. Robert Hovda, a contemporary representative of the liturgical tradition, notes this contrast of values when he asks:

> Where else [other than in the liturgy] in our society are all of us – not just a gnostic elite, but everyone – called to be social critics, called to extricate ourselves from the powers and principalities that claim to rule our daily lives in order to submit ourselves to the sole domination of the God before whom all of us are equal and where else are we all addressed and sprinkled and bowed to and sprinkled and incensed and touched and treated like some-body – all in the very same way? Where else are food and drink blessed and broken and poured out so that every-body, everybody shares and shares alike?[24]

Where else indeed? Where will the world look for a model of what a godly human community can be like? Certainly not to most modern corporations, where financial profit has the last word in making decisions about human value. Certainly not to the nation-states, where differences in power, ability, money, social standing determine a person's ultimate usefulness within the community. The liturgical tradition of spirituality argues that if the liturgical assembly can remain true to its calling, it will provide for the world at large the most visible sign of the way humans can be with one another that is godly and humane.

A COMMUNITY WITH PERMEABLE BOUNDARIES

We have seen the importance the liturgical tradition places on the unity of the Christian community, in its baptismal and eucharistic unity in Christ. Indeed that unity is of such a strength and resilience that neither time nor distance can rupture it; neither can create a boundary between those who are of one body with Christ. This means that when the tradition speaks about 'community', it is referring to something that is more than simply the visible society of those who happen to share a single temporal and spatial geography. As Evelyn Underhill puts it, when believers join in liturgical celebration they are accompanied by all Christians, past, present and future, who serve as our 'companions in the Way'. She continues: 'We are units in a mighty procession; and they can teach us how to walk.'[25]

The spirituality fostered by the liturgy, then, is a spirituality which encourages us to learn to walk with the dead. In the language of the liturgical tradition this is referred to as *anamnesis*, which is usually translated as 'remembering', but carries with it more the sense of the collapsing of the distance between 'then' and 'now' so that the redemptive acts of God are always present. In addition, we not only join our prayers to God in the liturgy with the 'communion of saints' living and dead, we also join with all of God's creation that has been singing praises to God from the beginning of time. In the words of the ancient eucharistic rite, we 'join with angels and archangels and all the company of heaven' in acclaiming the glory of God.[26]

It must not be overlooked that the Christian community has never accomplished the unity it so desires. Differences in history, belief, models of institutional life, and even in the forms and intentions of the liturgy, have created boundaries between and among the various branches of the Christian family. But in spite of this, the liturgical tradition has always found in the liturgy more to unite this family than there is to divide it. The spirituality which arises out of the common worship of the Church is a spirituality which is keyed to the deep union of voices raised in supplication, thanksgiving, rejoicing and intercession before God. We can see this expressed in the words of Alexander Schmemann, who says that within liturgical prayer,

> thinker and lover, sufferer and worker, Catholic and Quaker pool their resources. When we are confounded by sudden visions of holiness and self-abandonment beyond our span, our share in the Communion of Saints assures us that others will suffer and adore for us, and make up our deficiencies by their more abundant life. For since the life of the saints is the life of charity, they cannot keep anything for themselves alone. The Life by which they live is shared, communicated from one to another, as the sap of the Vine is given through the greater branches to the less.[27]

This emphasis in the tradition on the holiness of the community and its essential relationships might easily lead to a spirituality of 'insiders' and 'outsiders'. But this is not the case. For many within the tradition, the liturgy even has the power to erase the boundaries between those who are devout and those who are not. The anonymous author of *The Hermitage Within*, for example, tells the faithful that they must 'prefer liturgical prayer to private devotions, because whenever the liturgy is celebrated "through your lips, the whole world prays." You make up for the defection of those who do not pray, and through you the voice of love drowns that of sin.'[28]

But the 'permeability' of the community's boundaries is not

only a quality of the boundaries between varieties of Christian belief and practice and between the living and the dead, but between the community as a whole and the world. Again, it is the liturgy which becomes the model for this approach. Since, as an Anglican representative of the tradition observed, the liturgy is 'the continuous expression of the incarnation', it teaches us at every point that if we are to be united with God we must to be united with all those for whom Christ died.[29] The liturgical community as constituted by the liturgy is the ongoing, visible presence of Christ in the world, and must relate to that world in the same way that Christ related to it: over and over again this involved the breaking down of boundaries so that all people might become fully human.

As a result of this conviction, the liturgical tradition is particularly aware of the boundaries which have been placed around those who are marginalised by society: the poor, racial and ethnic minorities, the disabled, the powerless. In its contemporary expression, representatives of the liturgical tradition have been among the clearest voices for radical inclusion of all people in the mainstream of power, entitlement and decision-making. The place in which the outworking of this will be accomplished first, of course, is in the liturgy, where the voices of all people should be heard.

Indeed, many have gone so far as to say that whenever the voices of the poor and oppressed are absent from the liturgy, however beautiful, reverent and precise it may otherwise be, that liturgy is incomplete. This is not simply about 'democracy' or fairness, but about the meaning of the death and resurrection of Christ around which the liturgical assembly gathers. According to one contemporary representative of the tradition, it is from the presence of those on the margins of society, the 'strangers in our midst', that 'we will learn a language that has hitherto been unheard – a language that speaks of the vulnerability of the cross and the power of the resurrection'.[30] He continues in this vein: 'This gathering of many gifts – constituting many voices, many faces, many hands – enables the true nature of the church to be revealed in worship as bodying forth God's rule in the world.'[31] In other words, the liturgical tradition finds in the liturgy a clear and persistent call to remove any barrier which divides Christians from one another, which divides Christians from those believers who have gone before, which divides the community as a whole from those who strive to become what God intends them to be. And in the liturgy we are given the spiritual resources on which to draw as we attempt to make this happen.

THE FUTURE OF COMMUNITY

> Our entrance into the presence of Christ... is not an escape from the world, rather it is the arrival at a vantage point from which we can see more deeply into the reality of the world.
>
> Alexander Schmemann

If in the liturgy we find the tools for building a model of true community, we also find the tools for understanding the goal of that community, its future. Many within the tradition look to the etymology of the word 'liturgy' itself for a sense of what that goal and future might be. In Greek, the word *leitourgia* originally meant a 'public work', a work which some people perform for or on behalf of the larger society, a benefaction. Alexander Schmemann claims that the liturgy is a model for the whole of the Church's life: 'The church as a whole is "leitourgia" – a work for the sake of others.'[32] To be a part of the liturgical assembly, then, is to commit oneself to a community that has a trajectory which aims at God's eternity:

> [T]o take part in any liturgy is to signify to oneself and others that one is constituting a community and oneself as a member of that community. So to take part in the Christian liturgy is to take on one's role in a new kingdom, one that 'shall have no end'.[33]

To 'take on one's role in a new community,' a community which is itself a *leitourgia*, is to commit oneself to a particular way of being Christian. It is a commitment to participate in forming a community which will be a sign (a 'sacrament') to the world of what a true human community is meant to be, both by how it orders itself internally and by how it acts toward the world at large.

This is Christian worship stretching toward its 'eschatological fulfillment', and stretching Christian worshippers toward a vision of a common life that is both humane and godly. It is always acknowledged, of course, that our ordinary church services will never be an accurate reflection of a human community perfectly restored in Christ. But, as Anglican liturgist Paul Bradshaw points out, by allowing the liturgy to guide us, we are able to maintain our 'eschatological vigilance'.[34]

Some wish to relate this to the correspondence between the earthly and the heavenly liturgy. Although particularly associated with the Orthodox branch of liturgical spirituality (it was John Chrysostom who said of the Eucharist, 'For what do I care about heaven when [by partaking of the Lord's Supper] I have become heaven?'[35]), it is also found in the liturgical spirituality of many contemporary liberation theologians as well. Sri Lankan Tissa Balasuryia proposes:

> In the heavenly liturgy, all people of good will take part. There are no distinctions of the visible and the invisible church in heaven; all participate in singing 'a hymn to the Lord's glory.' We must try, within limits, to realize here on earth the universal dimensions of the one liturgy while maintaining its oneness in Christ Jesus.[36]

The community for which we strive, then, the 'true community' as God intends it to be, will be the community that gathers around the table at the 'heavenly banquet' to which the liturgy itself looks forward, and a time when 'Worship and service are one. Activity and rest will find harmony.'[37]

In commenting on the worship described in the Book of Revelation (Revelation 22:3–5), Canadian theologian David Newman says:

Worship continues but something remarkable has happened to it. The order of worship is no longer a hierarchy of a servant bowing to a master. The servant has become sovereign ruling over everything. Worship as metaphor for gospel is transformed from service into sovereign freedom, from work into play. It is the 'eschatological game' in which the saved and reconciled community live out their relationship with the God who no longer rules over them, but 'dwells with' them. There is no dichotomy between praise and empowerment. Praise is now the acknowledgement of the origin of freedom and, therefore, the source of the empowerment that flows from worship. Worship is a celebration of freedom.[38]

This does not imply that the liturgical tradition encourages a persistent liturgical otherworldliness. Even among Orthodox and Eastern Rite representatives of the tradition, for whom the liturgy in church is seen to be a reflection of the liturgy that takes place in heaven, the extent to which this reflection has been an accurate one is only known by looking at what happens when the members of that community are scattered in the world after the *leitourgia* that takes place in church is finished. For the liturgical tradition, the shape of the community is modelled *both* on the liturgy as it is and on this vision of the liturgy as it will be.

How does the liturgy form a spirituality which makes participation in and formation of this kind of true community possible? It does so, according to the liturgical tradition, by setting out images which shape a holy imagination, an imagination that can envision a joyful and humane future under God. It does so by becoming a safe and secure arena within which the courageous interaction with others, both inside and outside the community, is fostered. It does so by ritualising healthy and non-exploitative relationships, in which being known by others is never dangerous. It does so by giving the members of the community words by which to share their joy and lament, and by setting out a pattern of feasting and fasting by which we are able to rejoice and to weep with others. It does so by embodying a kind of 'godly optimism', which tells us that we can, indeed, strive for such a community, and that God will always be present to assist us in this holy endeavour. It is in the confidence that all this is true and operative in the liturgy that Alexander Schmemann can write that the journey toward the formation of a new kind of community begins 'when Christians leave their homes and beds'.

> The journey begins when Christians leave their homes and beds. They leave, indeed, their life in this present and concrete world, and whether they have to drive fifteen miles or walk a few blocks, a sacramental act is already taking place, an act which is the very condition of everything else that is to happen. For they are now on their way to constitute the *Church*. Or to be more exact, to be transformed into the Church of God. They have been individuals . . . they have been in the 'natural' world and a natural community. And now they have been called . . . to be more than what they were: a new community with a new life.[39]

4. LOCATING OURSELVES IN TIME AND SPACE

Christ yesterday and today, the beginning and the end,
the Alpha and the Omega, all time belongs to him and
all ages; to him be the glory and power through every
age together.

Words for the marking of the
Paschal Candle at the Easter Vigil

The fact that human beings have physical bodies is one of the
primary determiners of our spiritual lives. To be 'embodied'
means to be conditioned by the realities of both time and space,
to be subject to both gravity and history. And so the question
arises, how does our attitude toward time and space colour
our relationship with God? How do we locate ourselves in time
and space so that both of these realities become resources
for spiritual reflection and insight? The history of Christian
theology has made it clear that we are not simply spiritual
beings 'trapped' for a season in the physical world, but that
our bodies and our histories are integral parts of our relationship with God. But for Christian spirituality it has been a
particular challenge to understand what it means to be time-
bound and place-bound, and at the same time to strive for
godly living in the presence of the Eternal God.

TIME AND THE LITURGICAL TRADITION

Time has become a particular problem for those who are
seeking to build integrated spiritual lives in the contemporary
situation. The apocalyptic millennialism which has attended

the turning of the new century, the overwhelming sense of what Alexander Schmemann describes as 'the nightmarish alternation between rush and relaxation',[1] the vague feeling that we do not have a real stake in either our past or our future: all of these give time an ambiguous quality, both friend and enemy. The search for a usable past and a usable future, and for a relationship with time that will not leave us stranded 'out of time', has led many people to seek out rhythms of life and attitudes toward time which are healthy and sane.

The liturgical tradition of spirituality has always given a significant amount of its attention to this question of time as an aspect of our relationship with God. For representatives of this tradition, the liturgy of the Church not only embodies a particular spirituality of time, but also encourages particular patterns of time-keeping which are liberating rather than confining. The tradition is clear that to keep time with the liturgy is to avail ourselves of a rich treasury of words, gestures, symbols and rituals, which are designed to bring meaning to the times of our lives. In this way, the liturgy becomes a primary resource for the task of integrating our relationship with time into the overall fabric of our lives.

But we must be prepared to think of time in quite a new way if we follow this tradition. To enter into the spirit of the liturgy is to enter into a world in which time is much less linear and rigid, much more 'maleable', than in our ordinary experience. Indeed, time itself is collapsed into what has been called the 'eternal present'. As one contemporary representative of the tradition says of liturgical commemoration of past events:

> To commemorate is not to stand afar off from what happened in the past; on the contrary, it is to eliminate the distance between present and past. To commemorate is to give the past a new existence; it is to think that each of us is contemporaneous with historical events whose consequences we still endure or whose effects we still prolong in time.[2]

And so, when the pious Jew says at the Passover seder, 'God brought *me* out of Egypt', when the pious Christian says at the Lord's Supper, 'The Body of Christ is given on the Cross for *me*,' hope and memory and human history converge into a saving moment in the present nourished by a confident vision of the future.

Because of this capacity of the liturgy to 'eliminate the distance between past and present', the tradition is clear that in our worship we become one with Christians across time. Pope Leo the Great (d. 461), in a sermon for Christmas in about the year 450, makes this observation. He points to the various elements of the liturgical life and to their power to draw together Christians in all times and places:

> Although every individual that is called has its own order, and all the sons of the Church are separated from one another by intervals of time, yet, as the entire body of the faithful being born in the font of baptism is crucified with Christ in his Passion, raised again in his resurrection, and placed at the Father's right hand in his ascension, so with him they are born in his Nativity.[3]

Of course we are not only united to one another through this liturgical 'collapsing of history', we are also united to Jesus Christ, who becomes the model for the transcending of temporal constraints. Seventeenth-century poet and pastor George Herbert writes about the spiritual benefits of keeping the Lenten fast:

> Who goeth in the way which Christ hath gone,
> Is much more sure to meet with him, than one
> That travelleth byways.[4]

The times and seasons of the liturgy also have the capacity to bring our attention to the present time, the time in which we live, to understand the present as a gift from God, with its own demands and requirements:

> Worship expresses the mystery of the givenness of time

in a world in which the law of time is experienced as time inevitably passing away. To receive the gift of time is to experience grace over against the law of the passage of time; it is to have free time – a time within which human beings have the freedom for that quality of life known as *agape* (love) ... Christian worship participates in transcendence, not apart from, but in the midst of, worldly living. It does so by means of metaphors that express both the connection and the disjunction of this world with the beyond.[5]

Our responsibility for the present rests in this knowledge that, in the words of one contemporary representative of the tradition, '[w]e are always between morning and evening, between Sunday and Sunday, between Easter and Easter, between the two comings of Christ'.[6]

Past, present and future: the liturgical tradition takes all of these into account as it seeks models, insights and patterns of living by which we might construct an overall attitude toward time. It also takes account of the various aspects of the liturgy itself. Many representatives of the tradition have given sustained attention to the overall vision of time embodied in the words of the Church's corporate prayer;[7] others look to the spirituality of time embedded in the liturgy's own time-keeping system; still others ask probing questions about what it means for our understanding of time that the Church centres its present and future life on the words of a very ancient text. Out of this, as we shall see, a distinctive spirituality of time begins to emerge.

HEARING THE WORD OF GOD

What happens when we hear the Scriptures read in the liturgical assembly? Can these ancient texts somehow become the Living Word of God for those who listen? The liturgy certainly seems to operate on the assumption that it can. Dietrich

Bonhoeffer, writing about the way in which Scripture acts on faithful hearers in the worship service, says:

> We become part of what once took place for our salvation. Forgetting and losing ourselves, we, too, pass through the Red Sea, through the desert, across the Jordan into the promised land. With Israel we fall into doubt and unbelief and through punishment and repentance experience again God's help and forgiveness. All this is not mere reverie, but holy, godly reality. We are torn out of our own existence and set down in the midst of the holy history of God on earth.[8]

To proclaim the Word of God, then, forges a new community which stands in a new relation to time and history.

The way that the liturgical tradition has usually described this new relationship is centred on the difference between two different understandings of time itself; and these two understandings are summed up in the two Greek words *chronos* and *kairos*. *Chronos* denotes time that moves in a linear way from the beginning of time to the end, each minute, hour, week and year succeeding the next, each one the same in its essential quality. *Kairos*, on the other hand, is time which is suffused with meaning, it is *significant* time, time related to the saving work of God in Christ. Seen through the eyes of faith, each moment becomes a *kairos* event, a point in time which is for ever changed by the life, death and resurrection of Jesus Christ. As a contemporary representative of the tradition says: 'Every moment of chronological time is now the precious present in which eternal values are being communicated. The liturgy, under the influence of the Spirit, examines the teaching and example of Jesus from this contemplative perspective.'[9]

This does not mean that the Word of God never addresses us as a challenge, or judgement, or call to repentance; it does mean that each time we hear the Scripture read it is a *kairos* moment for us, a decisive moment. When we read the Scriptures as the dialogue between a community and its God we declare that the Lord's time of grace is *now*, and that all relationships with time which are exploitative are undermined. This means that time, instead of being something which confines and restricts the soul, now has the power to liberate and release it. As the reading of Scripture takes place, the liturgy becomes a 'laboratory of freedom', in which we find a new identity in relation to the saving work of God, past, present and future.

THE LITURGICAL SPIRITUALITY OF THE CHRISTIAN WEEK

Although the direct historical relationship between Christian and Jewish time-keeping is still the subject of debate among liturgical scholars, much of the liturgical spirituality surrounding the liturgical rhythm of the Christian week arises from the spirituality which has attended the keeping of Sabbath in Judaism. As Abraham Joshua Heschel argues, the Sabbath is in time what sacred places are in space: 'Judaism teaches us to be attached to holiness in time . . . the Sabbaths are our great cathedrals and our holy of holies, a shrine that neither the Romans nor the Germans were able to burn.'[10] For the faithful Jew, Sabbath comprises multiple meanings, rest, creation, liberation; it looks back to the origins of the world and forward to its culimination in God's reign of peace and justice:

> Sabbath marked creation's natural end, as if on that day a sort of circle was closed, since everything God had planned took shape in the whole we call the universe. In Jewish law and lore, the Sabbath has always stood, therefore, for wholeness, peace, and absence from want. Petitionary prayer, for example, is removed from the Sabbath liturgy, for who could possibly want for anything on that day?[11]

Over and over again we see these themes returning in the liturgical tradition when it thinks about the meaning of its principal day of worship. Sunday takes on much of the Sabbath imagery of beginnings and endings, initiation and completion. As one very early representative of the tradition declares, describing the place of Sunday in the spiritual economy of the Christian life, 'Sunday, indeed, is the day on which we all hold our common assembly, inasmuch as it is the first day on which God, transforming the darkness and matter, created the universe; and on the same day our Savior Jesus Christ rose from the dead.'[12]

Sundays, then, are the celebration of all that God has done, both in creation and in redemption. The blessings of Sunday are multiple, and representatives of the tradition often rise to lyric expressiveness when describing the place of Sunday in the life of the Christian. George Herbert, who can perhaps be called the tradition's 'poet laureate', describes Sundays as 'the pillars . . . on which heav'n's palace arched lies'. He goes on to say:

> The Sundays of man's life,
> Threaded together on time's string,
> Make bracelets to adorn the wife of the eternal glorious
>   King.
> On Sunday heaven's gate stands ope;
> Blessings are plentiful and rife,
> More plentiful than hope.[13]

Sunday, for Herbert, is not only a joyful occasion, but a gateway between earth and heaven, between time and eternity. And through this 'gateway', God's blessings pour out on the community at prayer.

The celebration of the Jewish Sabbath has also been centred on rest from labour, heightening the theme of liberation by its call for the cessation from all work, and linking Sabbath to the first Passover which celebrated the release from slavery in Egypt. Heschel writes:

> Labor is a craft, but perfect rest is an art. It is the result of an accord of body, mind, and imagination . . . the seventh

day is a palace in time, which we build. It is made of soul,
of job and reticence. In its atmosphere a discipline is a
reminder of adjacency to eternity.[14]

In its origins, the Christian Sunday had none of the overtones
of rest from labour that were a part of the Jewish Sabbath,
and indeed many Christians have been deeply suspicious of
strict Sabbath-keeping. Martin Luther declared: 'If anywhere
the day is made holy for the mere day's sake, then I order you
to work on it, ride on it, feast on it, to do anything to remove
this reproach from Christian liberty.'[15] But among certain
bodies of Christian believers (for example, the Reformed and
Puritan Protestants), Sunday rest in imitation of the Sabbath
has been an important theme. And the theme of liberty
remains strong within the tradition more generally, for whom
Sunday becomes the 'template' of our liberation: 'But ours is
the long day's journey of the Saturday. Between the suffering,
aloneness, unutterable waste on the one hand and the dream
of liberation, of rebirth, on the other.'[16]

Although we think of Protestant sabbatarianism as rigid
and austere, many modern exponents of the liturgical tradition
are suggesting that for the sake of developing a healthy attitude toward time we should begin to reconsider the keeping
of Sabbath days. Overworked people need rest.

> And they need to be reminded that they do not cause the
> grain to grow and that their greatest fulfilment does not
> come through the acquisition of material things. Moreover,
> the planet needs a rest from human plucking and burning
> and buying and selling. Perhaps, as Sabbath keepers, we
> will come to live and know these truths more fully, and
> thus to bring their wisdom to the common solution of
> humanity's problems.[17]

Others in the tradition look to the weekly celebration of the
Eucharist as a model for the establishment of a new relationship with time. In the Lord's Supper, 'distances, both temporal
and spatial are collapsed, as ritual contact is made with past,

present and future at once, and "this place" is united with "everywhere else"'. Indeed, 'all the boundaries are crossed: between individual and group; death and life; spirit and body; meaning and fact; beginning, lasting, and ending; old and new; here and everywhere; eternal and temporal; linear and cyclical time; host and guest; God and humankind'.[18] The Eucharist reveals Sunday for what it is, and in so doing reveals the meaning of all time. Schmemann writes:

> By remaining one of the ordinary days and yet revealing itself through the Eucharist as the eighth and first day, [Sunday] gives all days their meaning. It made the time of this world a time of the end, and it made it also a time of the beginning.[19]

Of course liturgical prayer is not confined to one day in the week. The tradition of daily prayer has deep roots in the Christian tradition, and has been the source of reflection on the meaning of time for the liturgical tradition. Through the lens of the liturgy, the ordinary course of day and night become transparent to the saving activity of God. As the author of I Clement says, 'We see, beloved, that the resurrection was accomplished according to the time. Day and night make visible to us resurrection. Night goes to sleep, the day rises; the day departs, night follows.'[20] In making our prayers day and night we conform ourselves to the rising and setting of the sun, and in so doing are 'witnesses to Christ'.[21] Lutheran liturgist Philip Pfatteicher argues: 'Human experience of time is deepened and transformed by regular prayer in the evening and the morning.' He continues:

> We experience these times as proclamations of creation and of the death and resurrection of Christ. Time is no longer experienced as merely duration as the hours pass and the years slide by ... To sanctify time is to heighten our awareness of the eternal significance of each moment lived in time. Not a moment is to be wasted, for each is

an opportunity for some worthwhile deed – service of a needy neighbor, rest, pondering the work of God.[22]

Day and night, then, mark something more than just the inevitable progression of time from beginning to end, birth to death. Prayer at set times in the day inserts us into another kind of time. An Orthodox nun speaks this way:

> Above the rhythm of the day's prayer there arches the greater rhythm of the day by day, month by month conformity to the given pattern. Prayer is cumulative. The repetitive rhythmic recitation takes us up into the flow of centuries of tradition, out of the past into the present, and out of the present into the future. And, with this sense of timelessness within time, we are naturally drawn into the awareness of the transcendent, into the incomprehensible, no-time of God.[23]

CELEBRATING THE CHRISTIAN YEAR

A significant arena within which the liturgical tradition finds resources for the development of a liturgical spirituality of time is in the Christian year. 'The purpose and function of the church year is to provide a kind of template by which our lives are given a common shape and order.'[24] The calendar of feasts and fasts, times and seasons, is not designed to make some times holy that would otherwise be 'profane'. It is rather to sensitise us to the fact that all time is holy. To allow *some* times and seasons to be transparent to the saving work of God is an invitation to see *all* times and seasons as transparent to the saving work of God. The witness of the tradition about the spiritual benefits of the keeping of the Christian year is clear: 'The sacred calendar is no magical formula; it cannot protect us from all spiritual dryness and misdirection. Nevertheless, this calendar enables us to live – and to die – more readily as the people of God.'[25]

In the Christian year we situate ourselves within a new temporal structure, rooted in and centred on the passion and resurrection of Christ. This transforms not only our sense of time, but our sense of who we are in relation to God. American Episcopalian Alan Jones says of the season of Lent:

> We are *en route* to the Passion. The Palm Sunday liturgy plays it out for us in dramatic detail. It is then that we enter the great drama of Holy Week with its climax at the Three Great Days of Good Friday, Holy Saturday, and Easter Day. Lent transforms our drifting into pilgrimage.[26]

To speak in this way about the days and seasons of the Christian year means that each day becomes a *kairos* moment for the Church, a 'now' of salvation. The fact that we can say at Christmas, '*Today* Christ is born', on Good Friday, '*Today* Christ is crucified and my sins with him', at Easter, '*Today* Christ is risen, and I too am risen with Christ', gives a new dimension to our interaction with time, giving it an enormous spiritual potency. 'By thus releasing Time from the inexorable, linear logic of "before" and "after", liturgy creates a playful pool of subjunctive ("might be") potential, a flexible, repertoire of possibilities for living never previously imagined or considered.'[27]

In this way, the calendar also functions as a spiritual teacher, guiding us through the events of the saving work of God in such a way that they become a part of our present experience. It releases in us our deepest desires for God, and teaches us the path we must take to make those desires a reality:

> The Church's year celebrates and gives us the opportunity to deepen our wildest longings. Nothing need be left out. The cycle includes bad times as well as good. There is wounding and healing, dying and rising. We celebrate new beginnings and we give due honor to times for dying. This dying and rising, of fasting and feasting, corresponds to something deep within us. The latter provides occasions for rejoicing; the former helps us to clarify exactly what it is we are celebrating.[28]

If ordinary chronological time is like an arrow, moving inexorably from beginning to end, or like a circle, endlessly returning us to the same place to relive our mistakes over and over again, then time shaped by and infused with meaning by the liturgy is like a spiral. It is carrying us progressively toward the completion of God's plan and towards our own fulfilment. In a sermon on the New Year, Anglican Divine Lancelot Andrewes makes this point:

> Now at this time is the turning of the year ... Everything now turning that we would also make it our time to turn to God ... Repentance itself is nothing but a kind of circling ... which circle consists of two turnings ... First a turn wherein we look forward to God and with our whole heart resolve to turn to Him. Then a turn again wherein we look backward to our sins wherein we have turned from God ... The wheel turns apace, and if we turn not the rather these turnings may overtake us.[29]

THE END OF TIME

> To be deeply Christian is to know and to live out the conviction that the whole human family dwells continuously at the intersection of time and eternity.
>
> Lawrence Stookey[30]

Many representatives of the tradition suggest that for the formation of an adequate spirituality of time it is not sufficient to celebrate particular times and seasons, or even to allow liturgical prayer to make each moment of chronological time transparent to the love and mercy of God. They wish to point us toward a spirituality of time which sees all present time from the perspective of the final consummation of all things. Throughout much of the history of the liturgical tradition, this was expressed as a strong desire to keep time well on earth in order to mirror the time-keeping of heaven. By ensuring that the rhythms of the liturgy were completely synchronised with the movements of the stars and planets, the Christian believer and the Church could participate in God's eternity.

Marianne Sawicki argues that resurrection 'ruptures temporality' and that remembering the resurrection in the liturgy has the same effect – in participation in the liturgy we 'cross the eschatological frontier'.[31] Such an eschatological approach 'recognizes the vicissitudes and emptiness of chronological time. It also recognizes that we and the whole creation will "pass away". Therefore, the eschatological approach seeks to hear the "last word", the word which will not pass away.'[32]

One might think that this approach to time would lead to moral complacency and inertia. On the contrary, for the liturgical tradition of spirituality this understanding of time sets us up for action in and for the world. It gives a special urgency to the exigencies of daily living: 'The experience of time as beginning and end gives an absolute importance to whatever we do now, makes it final, decisive. The experience of time as beginning fills all our time with joy, for it adds to it the "coefficient of eternity".'[33] 'We seek the "last word" of Christian eschatology which will transform both the "meantime" and the "end time" of our lives.'[34]

> What seems like the beginning, set long ago in the distant past, is in fact a promise and guarantee of what is to come. We live always on the horizon of divine promise, and that perspective casts doubt on all our comfortable security here. We learn anew that we are at most resident aliens in a foreign land, 'strangers and foreigners . . . seeking a homeland' (Hebrews 11:13–16).[35]

An eschatological spirituality rooted in the liturgical vision of time and eternity allows us to take the risk of deep human encounter 'in the meantime' knowing that the 'end time' is secure. In addition, we can sit lightly on all of those things which bind us and give us a sense that our ultimate security rests in our own hands. Time, then, for the liturgical tradition of Christian spirituality is ultimately to be seen as a vehicle for the liberation of humanity, and for our participation in the compassionate mission of God.

A LITURGICAL SPIRITUALITY OF PLACE

> For a believer, the church shares in a different space from
> the street on which it stands. The door that opens on the
> interior of the church actually signifies a dissolution of
> continuity. The threshold that separates the two spaces
> also indicates the distance between two modes of being,
> the profane and the religious. The threshold is the limit,
> the boundary, the frontier that distinguishes and opposes
> two worlds – and at the same time the paradoxical place
> where those worlds communicate, where passage from the
> profane to the sacred world becomes possible.
>
> Mircea Eliade[36]

> To the Glory of God this Cathedral burned, 14th November
> 1940.
>
> Inscription at the threshold of Coventry Cathedral

'To be rooted', said the philosopher Simone Weil, 'is perhaps
the most important and least recognized need of the human
soul.' Our attitude toward the various kinds of places and
spaces in our lives expresses this deeply felt human need.
Places where we live and pray and where significant things
have happened are important to us. We are willing to fight for
them; sometimes we are even willing to die for them. The very
fact that people can talk meaningfully about 'sacred space'
attests to the singular role of places in the divine–human
relationship.

But space, like time, has become something of a problem for
those who seek to discover resources for the spiritual life in
the contemporary world. Jewish theologian Elie Weisel
describes us as a generation of 'displaced persons', who have
generally chosen mobility over stability and who have nowhere
to call 'home'. Urban nomadism, suburban isolation, the
despoiling of the environment, the uncertainties of the geography of cyberspace: all of these make our human task of
becoming 'rooted' extremely difficult in the twentieth century.
As a result of these difficulties, conversation about the ways

in which we might negotiate our relationship with places has been occurring within and among all of the various traditions of Christian spirituality.

Because of its deep concern with both the physical setting of the liturgy and with the future of places and spaces in God's economy, the liturgical tradition has added its own distinctive voice to this conversation. What does the liturgy itself say about the various places we inhabit? What is the devotional meaning of the environment within which the worship of the Christian community is celebrated? How do those places we have traditionally wanted to define as 'sacred spaces' relate to the wider physical geography? What does the 'landscape of praise' tell us about the wider 'landscape' of our spiritual lives? Wherever we encounter the representatives of the liturgical tradition, we find them asking these kinds of questions as they seek, for themselves and for others, 'to be rooted' as a part of the overall nourishment of the spiritual life.

But this being said, for the liturgical tradition of Christian spirituality there is an essential ambiguity embedded deep within this question of the role of places within our spiritual life, an ambiguity which is highlighted by the two quotations at the head of this section. We are indeed tied to our geographies and shaped by our places, but over and over again the tradition invites us to ask, 'Are we human beings truly at home in the world of spaces and places, or does our true home (and our true nature) have nothing about it that can be thought of in geographical terms?' Within this ambiguity about the spiritual value of places, which traces its origins all the way back to the Bible, the liturgical tradition takes various approaches to the problem of 'locating' ourselves, and of understanding and appropriating physical geography as an aspect of our relationship with God and others.

THE ENVIRONMENT FOR WORSHIP AS METAPHOR FOR THE SPIRITUAL LIFE

For the liturgical tradition of Christian spirituality, the physical environment for worship provides a rich source of imagery for understanding the relationship with God. At the roots of this approach lies Paul's vibrant architectural analogy for the holy life: that Christians are to see their body as the 'temple of the Holy Spirit', its dwelling-place and home. In another passage, he refers to the domestic preparations made for the Jewish Passover seder when he says that, just as the house of the pious Jew is cleansed of old leaven before the Passover feast, so the Christian life has had the 'leaven of malice and evil' cleansed from it in Christ, who is the Passover Lamb (1 Corinthians 5:6–8). In a fourth-century sermon, Augustine follows this method when he points to his surroundings and says to those gathered for worship, 'This is our house of prayer, but we too are a house of God. If we are a house of God, its construction goes on in time so that it may be dedicated at the end of time.'[37]

There is a reciprocal relationship between the imagery of the Christian life and the liturgical environment. Just as the believer is to be imagined as being 'built' into a holy temple, so too is the 'temple' to be built on the model of the holy Christian life. These images are reinforced in the rites by which church buildings are dedicated to their purpose as settings for the liturgical life of the community. Philip Pfatteicher writers:

> The rite of dedication of a church as it is prescribed in both East and West underscores the similarity between the church building and the individual human body. The dedication treats the building as if it were a living person undergoing baptism, sprinkling it with water and anointing its walls with oil.[38]

For Eastern Orthodox representatives of the liturgical tradition, the church building carries yet another layer of

spiritual meaning. In addition to being a window onto the
reality of the Christian life, it is also a window onto the reality
of heaven. Each element of the liturgical space and its furnishings partakes of the analogy: the ceiling is the vault of
heaven, and is therefore painted with stars, clouds and angels;
the altar is the throne of God, surrounded with gilded canopies
and the icons of the saints. In this way the church building
participates in our *theosis*, our gradual divinisation. By setting
ourselves within the church building, which is the likeness of
heaven, we stimulate our transformation into the likeness
of God. And of course in participating in the liturgy we participate in the song that is sung before the face of God throughout
eternity.

If the church building itself provides a central metaphor
for understanding the nature of the soul's progress toward
godliness, then the way we *interact*, physically, with the church
building also encourages spiritual insight. To gather around
table, font and pulpit, to walk the journey to Calvary marked
by the Stations of the Cross, to kneel in prayer surrounded by
the remains of those who have died in the fellowship of Christ:
in each of these actions we expand our range of images for the
relationship with God as our bodies rehearse the gestures of
holiness. Philip Pfatteicher is also concerned with describing
what takes place when we allow ourselves to move intention-
ally within a building, when we allow the building to be a part
of the process of seeking spiritual depth and integrity. Here
he is discussing the great labyrinth which is laid into the floor
of the centre aisle of the cathedral at Chartres:

> The meaning of the labyrinth is uncertain, or more likely
> manifold . . . Entering the labyrinth was the equivalent of
> an initiation. The center could be a safe city, a tomb, a
> sanctuary or other magical-religious space that must be
> protected against the uninitiated. Pilgrims who enter the
> church from the west and move unobstructed toward
> the altar in the east must pass over the labyrinth on the
> way. They are thus reminded that safe arrival at the goal,

a place difficult of access and well-defended, is by means of a trial in which not everyone may triumph. The way is straight and narrow, is arduous and fraught with peril, for it is a passage from the profane to the sacred, from illusion to reality, from the temporal to the eternal.[39]

To allow the space within which we worship to aid us in imagining the possibilities of the spiritual life, and to allow the spiritual life to aid us in imagining the possibilities of the space within which we worship is to follow a central insight of the liturgical tradition of Christian spirituality. Those seeking holiness are invited to see the Christian life as a spiritual geography; and thus to take heed of the 'godly admonition' of the writer of 1 Peter, who encourages his hearers: 'like living stones, let yourselves be built into a spiritual house' in which 'spiritual sacrifices acceptable to God through Jesus Christ are offered' (1 Peter 2:5).

SPACE AS TEACHER OF SPIRITUAL TRUTH

The environment for worship also functions as a spiritual teacher and guide for those within this tradition. In a hymn written in the middle of the nineteenth century, the Danish pastor and poet Nikolai F. S. Grundtvig describes the way in which the various liturgical furnishings of the Church draw the worshipper toward spiritual insight:

> The font stands here before our eyes
>   telling us how God received us;
>   the altar recalls Christ's sacrifice
> and what his table provides us . . .

Other elements in the church building have also been understood to function in this pedagogical way for the liturgical tradition. Elizabethan Bishop John Jewel, as he argues against the desire of some to remove images from the interior of church buildings, reaches back into the tradition to remind his readers that:

St. Gregory calleth them the laymen's books; and the fathers in a later council say: 'We may learn more in a short while by an image than by long study and travail in the Scriptures.' And for the same cause St. Basil compareth an image painted with a story written.[40]

Although it is quite commonplace to find such things as stained glass and other forms of religious iconography spoken of as 'catechesis for the illiterate', for medieval proponents of the liturgical tradition visual imagery was more than simply a delivery system for religious education. The complex and subtle relationship between what is seen and the spiritual life in this period rests on a particular kind of 'theological optics' which was a feature of medieval philosophy. When a person looked at something, it was believed that the visual image passed through the centre of the eye and imprinted itself upon the soul of the viewer. So the various forms of visual and plastic arts were not placed within the church building simply for the purpose of edification, or even inspiration; what one saw had the potential to shape the soul, to alter it permanently for better or for worse. If one looked upon godly images, the soul was edified; if one looked upon ungodly images, the soul was deformed.[41]

SPACE AS ENABLER OF OUR PRAYER

For the liturgical tradition, places are not only designed to provide metaphors, lessons and models for our devotional life, they also give added focus and potency to our prayer. Two poets help us here. T. S. Eliot speaks of the spiritual power which is derived from the act of praying 'where prayer has been valid',[42] and Philip Larkin describes the church building as the place which is 'proper to grow wise in' and which provokes in us a persistent 'hunger to be more serious'.[43] Having hallowed our spaces, the tradition suggests, our spaces in their turn hallow us:

[T]he Church building is consciously symbolic space which

heightens and enriches the Church's prayer in a unique
way: perhaps something like a concert hall, whose acous-
tics bring out resonances in the music which are lost in
any ordinary room, so that the sound is richer and truer.
A good concert hall enables the music to speak with a
special freedom and be more than usually true to itself. A
prayed-in church does the same for the prayers of those
who pray.[44]

Or, as one of the very earliest exponents of the traditions said:
'A place of prayer, the spot where believers assemble together,
is likely to have something gracious to help us.'[45]

It has been usual since the earliest centuries for Christians
to situate their church buildings so that the end in which the
altar is placed faces eastward. To 'orient' the church building
in this way is always understood to have both symbolic significance and spiritual value. 'Orientation,' says an Orthodox
theologian from India, 'or symbolic turning to the source of
light, to the sun of justice, to the original human experience
of communion with God, to the joyful light of the dawn of
resurrection, is a dynamic gesture that sets the community in
motion in a movement that constantly stretches forward.'[46] If,
then, the church building faces toward the rising of the sun,
so does the worshipper at prayer, 'as though the soul beheld
the rising of the True Light'.[47]

LITURGICAL SPACE AND OTHER GEOGRAPHIES

Many within the liturgical tradition are concerned with the
relationship between the space consecrated for the liturgical
prayer of the Church and the other kinds of spaces and places
in the world. At the very least, they would argue that by
designating *some* space as holy, as transparent to the glory of
God, we begin to open our eyes to the realisation that *all* space
is holy. Some wish to argue that the space in which we worship
serves as a beacon, a kind of 'leavening agent', for the sur-

rounding area. As the Bishop of Coventry said of his new cathedral in that city:

> This cathedral is set in the very midst of the teeming industrial and commercial life of the City of Coventry, not something apart from life on the circumference but rather placed at the very heart and kernel of life's activities, drawing them up through its worship and liturgy to God's very throne.[48]

For many this 'sacramental' function of the church building means that what happens within it must also be a visible sign of the love of God. In order to fulfil its spiritual function, the liturgical space must not be a source of division, but of reconciliation; not a place of the exercise of power, but for the exercise of mercy; not a place for the aggrandisement of the few, but a place for the care of the many.

For the ancient proponents of this tradition, however, liturgical prayer has a direct relationship to the ordering of a much wider geography. Beginning with the idea that the crucifixion is both the temporal and spatial centre of the world, they argue that four points of the compass are derived from the shape of the cross, and that in our prayer-posture we 'situate' ourselves at the symbolic centre of the world. In an ancient homily, Maximus of Turin (*c.* 381–*c.* 470) makes this clear:

> We pray with our hands outstretched like Christ's on the Cross, for by such a position we show forth the Passion of the Lord. Our prayer accompanied by this attitude will be the more quickly answered, for, in this manner, whole the soul speaks with Christ the body imitates the Crucified.[49]

Maximus then goes on to say that by the sign of the cross made by participants praying in the liturgy, we are 'reminded that the whole earth is divided into four' and that we stand at the turning-point of the world.

A FUSION OF TIME AND SPACE

But in all of this, the liturgical tradition of Christian spirituality is acutely aware that our ability to 'locate' ourselves spiritually is not ultimately a function of particular places and spaces, even those we designate as 'sacred spaces'. As Christians who derive their primary spiritual insight from the liturgy, they recognise that our spiritual geography is always centred on Christ, and that 'wherever two or three are gathered together' the Risen Christ is present. The assembly of Christian believers, then, wherever and whenever it is manifested, is the principal 'sacred space' for those within the liturgical tradition, and the shape of the relationships within the worshipping community becomes the leavening agent for the wider geography.

In addition, the liturgy affirms that all space is filled with the presence of Jesus Christ. As the Letter to the Ephesians puts it in its joyful hymn to the Ascension of Christ, 'He who descended is the same one who ascended so that he might fill all things' (Ephesians 4:10). A seventeenth-century representative of the tradition, George Herbert, reflects on this in another way, when he speaks of God's use of the liturgy to point us toward the reality of Christ's presence in the world:

> Man had straight forward gone
> To endless death; but thou dost pull
> And turn us round to look on one,
> Whom, if we were not very dull,
> We could not choose but look on still;
> Since there is no place so alone,
> That which he doth not fill.[50]

But the liturgical tradition does not wish us to stop there, since, as the liturgy constantly reminds us in words and images, we look forward to a time when all places will be transformed, when all places will fulfil their intended purpose as vehicles for our relationship with God. In the end neither 'here' nor 'now' is the true home of the disciple of Jesus Christ.

And it is in the liturgy, especially the liturgy of the Eucharist, that we stand 'with one foot in both places'. As Theodore of Mopsuestia states in an Easter homily: 'Since it is the signs of heavenly reality that [Christ] accomplishes in type, this sacrifice must likewise be a manifestation of it; and the bishop performs a kind of image [*eikon*] of the liturgy that takes place in heaven.'[51] Reinforcing the point, he goes on to say: 'Every time the liturgy ... is performed we must think of ourselves in our imagination as people present in heaven; by faith we sketch in our minds a vision of heavenly realities.'[52]

Because of this deep concern with the future of places in the spiritual life, time and space are ultimately intertwined with one another for those within the liturgical tradition of Christian spirituality. That intertwining is celebrated and revealed in the corporate worship of the Church, which says in word and action, 'There will be a time when space will be experienced like this; there will be a place when time will be experienced like this.' It is therefore not unusual to find that exponents of the tradition move between temporal categories and spatial categories, between here and now, there and then, with particular ease. Philip Pfatteicher concludes:

> Sacred space, marked out and enclosed by a church building, is a declaration of the paradox of a timeless proclamation embedded in time, the Eternal born in mortal flesh at a specific moment and in a particular geographic area. It is a window of heaven and a door to eternity carrying our sight and spirit beyond the confines of this world and into the next as far as the human spirit can penetrate and understand.[53]

Finally, it must be said that many people, having considered our spiritual history, have placed the blame for the current ecological crisis we face on this sense that we are not truly at home in this world. If there will ultimately be a 'new heaven and a new earth', and if this earth is not our true home, then care for the earth needs not be a very high priority. In his poem called 'Dwellings', William James Riley speaks of the 'ecstasy of those who dwell forever in a place our spirit knows as home'. At the same time, however, he also describes the breakdown of boundaries which mark the 'gateways between here and there' and without which 'one space is the same as any other'. He concludes by warning us: 'In a world without places, there is no responsibility for yesterday and tomorrow.' And it is precisely in its willingness to provide and to recognise those 'gateways between here and there', those places which become transparent to the presence of God in all places, that the liturgical tradition can provide us with such important resources not only for those seeking an ecologically sound spirituality, but for anyone seeking 'to be rooted' in a rootless time.

5. LIVING RESPONSIBLY

I am sure the Liturgy will torment us so long as we
continue selfish and divided, therefore I will cling to it.
I am sure it may be the instrument of raising us out of
our selfishness and divisions; therefore I value it above
all the artificial schemes of reconciliation, all philosophical
theories, all inventions, however skillful, for the
reconstruction of human society in which there
evidently lies no such power.

F. D. Maurice[1]

As the Preface to this series points out, spirituality concerns
'the whole of human life', it is about being in relationship with
God, with others, and with the created order as a whole. Our
actions and choices about what is 'right' within these relationships affect and are affected by our understanding of God and
of our innermost selves as we seek to become people of integrity
and righteousness. Conversely, not only are our actions rooted
in particular approaches to the spiritual life, but they also
have real spiritual consequences, not only for us but for others
as well. Even if we are not actively involved in ministries of
spiritual guidance, our behaviour can often be a window onto
the reality of God as people look at us and ask themselves,
'What can explain a life like that?'

How does the liturgical tradition of spirituality make the
essential link between Christian worship and the living out of
the Christian life in a humane and responsible manner? What
is the relationship between the words, images and actions of
our common prayer and moral and ethical decision-making?

In every age, representatives of the liturgical tradition have reflected on these questions, and have consistently stressed that the liturgy, as a whole and in its constituent parts, shapes people for godly living in various different ways. Giving us strength and visions of holiness, allowing us to model responsible behaviour and to express our contrition when we have failed to pattern our lives after that model: the corporate worship of the Church becomes the environment within which Christians discover what it means to be a moral being and how to live out of that understanding.

STRENGTH AGAINST TEMPTATION TO SIN

Q: 'What does baptizing with water signify?'
A: It signifies that the old Adam in us, together with all sins and evil lusts, should be drowned by daily sorrow and repentance and be put to death, and that the new man should come forth daily and rise up, cleansed and righteous, to live forever in God's presence.

Martin Luther, *Small Catechism*

For most forms of Christian spirituality, the conviction is strong that if we are to live holy and responsible lives we must continuously resist the temptation to sin, the temptation to turn away from God and follow (in the words of the Book of Common Prayer) the 'devices and desires of our own hearts'. And the liturgical tradition of Christian spirituality concurs. Despite holding a variety of opinions on the precise nature and consequences of human sin, all representatives of the tradition would agree with the words of K. E. Kirk who describes sin as 'that which impedes spiritual progress'.[2]

Perhaps the most ancient witness of the liturgical tradition about the relationship between common prayer and temptation to sin is that faithful participation in the liturgy provides an armour which protects us against evil, against all that would draw us away from God. Many would say that in the liturgy we are infused with the grace of God, the power of the Holy Spirit, the presence of the Risen Christ, precisely that we might have the strength to resist the temptation to sin when it comes. One of the very earliest representatives of the liturgical tradition, Ignatius of Antioch (d. *c.* 117), told a community of Christians in a letter, 'If you gather together frequently the power of Satan is undone and his deathly power over your faith is broken.'[3]

As the tradition progressed, one or another of the elements in common prayer was seen to be especially effective in the warfare with sin. For the writer of the thirteenth-century rule for Anchorites, the Ancrene Wisse, it is the Lord's Supper which has this potent power:

> This high sacrament, taken in firm faith, over all other things uncovers his [the Devil's] tricks and breaks his strength. Truly dear sisters, when you feel him near you, because you have firm faith, will you not merely laugh him loudly to scorn, that he is such an old fool that he comes to increase his own pain and to braid you a crown.[4]

The author's argument is that in the sacrament Christ comes to dwell within the believer, and that Christ and the Devil cannot occupy the same dwelling:

> Therefore, my dear sisters, hold yourselves upright in true faith. Firmly believe that all the devil's strength melts through the grace of that holiest of the sacraments, which you see as often as the priest says Mass – the virgin's child Jesus, God's son, who descended at those times in flesh to your inn and humbly takes his shelter within you.[5]

Or, as the fifth/sixth-century visionary Pseudo-Dionysius says (in a less anthropomorphic view of evil): 'One cannot participate in contradictory realities at one and the same time, and whoever enters into communion with the One cannot proceed to live a divided life. He must be firmly opposed to whatever may sunder this communion.'[6]

For most within the tradition, Christian initiation transmits this kind of power to guard against the temptation to sin.

In the ancient baptismal rites, the candidate made a formal renunciation of the Devil ('I renounce you, O Satan, and all your works, your pomp, and all your service'[7]), and this was seen as a powerful weapon in the Christian's spiritual armoury. John Chrysostom compares this renunciation to the blood on the door-posts of the Jews in captivity in Egypt:

> Moses' mission was to lead out from Egypt a persecuted people. Christ's to rescue all the people of the world who were under the tyranny of sin. There the blood of a lamb was a charm against the destroyer; here the blood of the Unspotted Lamb, Jesus Christ, is appointed your inviolable sanctuary against demons.

And the renunciation of the Devil in these ancient rites was followed by an anointing with oil. Chrysostom continues in his exposition, saying that with the oil of anointing, each of the newly baptised is 'now a soldier and have signed on for spiritual contest'.

Because the liturgy as a whole is an arena within which sin is taken seriously, the strengthening against the temptation to sin takes various forms. Washing and anointing with oil at baptism, receiving communion, rites of penance, and the various rituals of penitence, the petition for the prayers of the saints on our behalf: all of these have not only forensic but also medicinal effects on the believer. For all within the liturgical tradition, these words, rites, gestures infuse believers with the spiritual power necessary to combat temptation; in the Church's traditional language they are a 'remedy against sin', and therefore a necessary prerequisite for the moral life.

THE MORAL DEMANDS OF THE LITURGY

In addition to strengthening participants against the perennial temptation to draw away from God and from the godly life, the liturgy also makes its own specific, positive moral demands. We see in the liturgy that we are united with others, and that we are therefore responsible both *to* them and *for* them. Following in the direction which Paul set in the First Letter to the Corinthians, all representatives of the liturgical tradition of spirituality make this connection, emphasising, each in his or her particular way, the need for mutual care within the Christian community. John Chrysostom, referring to the relationship between the Lenten fast and the moral life, chastises his hearers for their behaviour:

> Do not limit the benefit of fasting merely to abstinence from food, for a true fast means refraining from evil; loose every unjust bond, put away your resentment against your neighbor, forgive him his offenses. Do not let your fasting lead to wrangling and strife. You do not eat meat, but you devour your brother, your sister; you abstain from wine, but not from insults![8]

To look at one another within the liturgical assembly is to see our brothers and our sisters; it is to see those who are bound together with us by bonds of mutual love, generosity and care.

We are reminded of this spiritual kinship in many and various ways in the liturgy. To offer the Kiss of Peace to one another, for example, is to commit ourselves to living within those bonds. As Augustine (354–430) tells his congregation:

> [We say] 'Peace be with you' and the Christians kiss one another with a 'holy kiss' (Rom. 16:16). This is a sign of peace. Let what lips express outwardly be also in the conscience, that is, as your lips draw nearer to your brother, so let your heart not withdraw from his.[9]

We are reminded of this spiritual kinship when we share in Holy Communion (and of course the Greek word which the English word 'communion' translates is *koinonia*, meaning fellowship or community), in the rites of foot-washing at the Maundy Thursday service, in our prayers of intercession and petition for one another. Over and over again, the liturgy sends this message about the need for right relationships within the worshipping community, and over and over again the liturgical tradition invites us to hear that message.

THE LITURGY AND ETHICS IN THE WIDER COMMUNITY

Most within the tradition are clear that the liturgy also makes demands on our behaviour within the wider network of relationships of which we are a part. In baptism we commit ourselves to bearing the image of Christ so that others might know the love of God. In our intercessory prayer we not only ask God to intervene in the situations for which we pray, we commit ourselves to intervening in those situations ourselves. When we offer one another signs of the Peace of Christ, we commit ourselves to do all we can to reconcile with all those whom we have wronged. The liturgy even reminds us to pray 'for all who hate us', acknowledging the truth of the ancient saying: 'We can love God only as much as we love our worst enemy.'

But for those within the liturgical tradition, this connection between ethics and liturgy is most clearly seen in the eucharistic rites: in the Lord's Supper we see a model for the humane treatment of all people. 'Do you wish to honour the Body of Christ?' John Chrysostom tells his congregation in a famous sermon on the Eucharist:

> Do not despise him where he is naked. Do not honor him here in the church building with silks, only to neglect him outside, where he is suffering from cold and from nakedness. For he who said, 'This is my Body,' is the same who said 'you saw me, a hungry man, and you did not give me to eat.' Of what use is it to load the table of Christ? Feed the hungry and then come and decorate the Table. You are making a golden chalice and you do not give a cup of cold water? The Temple of your afflicted brother's body is more precious than this Temple (the Church). The Body of Christ becomes for you an altar. It is more holy

than the altar of stone on which you celebrate the holy sacrifice. You are able to contemplate this altar everywhere
in the street and in the open squares.[10]

The grace of God which is available to us in the liturgical
assembly, the awareness it fosters of the mercy and kindness
with which God has approached us, calls us toward the holiness of life, holy relationships with others, and a gentle and
peaceable approach to the wider creation.[11]

This also includes the right and holy use of our money and
our possessions. For many within this tradition, the act of
liturgical offering, both the offering bread and wine for the
Lord's Supper and offering money for the support of the
Church and its ministries, invites us to see to the material
aspects of our lives in a particular way. To offer to God the
fruit of our labour is to acknowledge that all that we have
ultimately comes from God and ultimately belongs to God. It
is also to allow our material lives to be taken by God, blessed
by God, and transformed by God into something holy, something that will enable others to know the mercy and goodness
of God. In this way the liturgy makes a stand against greed,
exploitation and the use of goods and money in ways which
divide people from one another.[12]

In the liturgy we are also invited to be 'present' to one
another, not only to those within the community, but to all
whom we encounter. 'Worship', says American Franciscan
Regis Duffy, ' . . . does not refer to rituals, but to the symbolized
experience of God's presence, contesting our lack of presence.'[13]

> Presence is, of course, more than attention. It is self-gift
> and enabling love . . . Such religious symbols initiate a
> process of conflict and change because God calls us to re-
> examine the purpose of our lives and the use of our time.
> Religious symbols are God's practical way of inviting us
> to assess the current position of our lives and the new
> commitments that may be needed.[14]

Many exponents of this tradition claim that the ability to be

truly 'present', to attend without distraction to what is in front
of us, and to accept the demands of commitment that this
makes, may be one of the greatest spiritual lessons the liturgy
has to teach.

For one religious group which is well represented in the
liturgical tradition, the Society of Friends, this kind of attentive presence is best achieved through the experience of
liturgical silence, which is seen to be the necessary foundation
of all responsible action. To eliminate the 'chatter' in our lives
enables us to hear the voice of God planted deep within, and
allows us to hear the claims God lays on our behaviour. And
silence has another function in the development of holy
relationships with others. In silence, Friends claim, in the
renunciation of words, we confess that we do not have the final
word about the world and its destiny. In a world where human
words are so often used to control, to dominate, to manipulate,
perhaps to be truly human is not to speak but rather to listen,
to listen in silence to that Word of Peace planted deep within
the human soul.

SOCIAL RESPONSIBILITY

Many within the liturgical tradition of Christian spirituality
say that the liturgy is not only the source for the formation of
personal morality, but the stimulus and model for all social
and political action as well. In a sense, in thinking about the
liturgy in relation to Christian morality in this way, those
within the liturgical tradition are following the direction set
by the Old Testament prophet Amos. In the fifth chapter of
the Book of Amos, God chastises the errant Israel:

> I hate, I despise your festivals,
> and I take no delight in your solemn assemblies.
> Even though you offer me your burnt offerings and grain
>   offerings,
> I will not accept them;
> and the offerings of well-being of your fatted animals

> I will not look upon.
> Take away from me the noise of your songs;
> I will not listen to the melody of your harps.
> But let justice roll down like waters,
> and righteousness like an ever-flowing stream.[15]

In other words, no matter how ornate, ritually correct and aesthetically beautiful the worship of Israel may be, if it is not matched by a commitment to the establishment of just and righteous relationships in the world, it is worthless in the sight of God. Most within the liturgical tradition of Christian spirituality would say that the same is true of Christian worship as well. But in a more positive sense, the liturgical tradition is also clear that there are rich resources within the common prayer of the Church for our social ethic.

The link between social justice and the liturgy has roots deep within the tradition's history, and is reclaimed whenever the tradition recognises that Christians have a moral responsibility for the quality of the social and political systems which determine the quality of life for our neighbours near and far. At these times the liturgy is seen as a principal agent for sensitising people to issues of intolerance, poverty, inequity of resource distribution, and also as the arena within which the liturgical assembly is strengthened and empowered for active involvement in putting an end to unjust social structures. This connection between Christian common prayer and Christian social action is especially clear among the English 'Sacramental Socialists' of the nineteenth century, the American 'Social Gospel Movement' in the early 1900s, and the various liberation theologies (including feminist theology) of the twentieth century.

The liturgy challenges all divisions based upon class, race, gender, ethnicity. As F. M. Garrett, one of the earliest of the 'Sacramental Socialists', says:

> If the unity of Humanity is shown at the altar to be truth, it must influence business, society, politics. The class divisions into which Society is split up are no longer tolerable

when they are seen to contradict that unity which is the ground of all real communion in Christ.[16]

This involves not only all inequitable social structures, but all inequitable distribution of resources based on those structures. The blessing of the bread at communion is intimately related to all other bread in the world, and the giving of the bread to communicants is related to the availability of all bread. One contemporary representative of the tradition echoes the words of the prophet Amos: 'To thank God for what is stolen from the poor is monstrous hypocrisy ... Perhaps we will not have so much trouble thanking God for food ... on the day that it is equitably distributed around the planet.'[17]

Indeed, the 'materiality' of the liturgy, and particularly of the liturgy of the Lord's Supper, challenges the way we think of and use *all* material goods. For many within the liturgical tradition, the breaking of bread in the Eucharist cries out against the way we turn the creation committed to our care into weapons of power and destruction.[18] As Kenneth Leech writes:

> This bread is not some special religious bread; it is bread which has been through the industrial process, bread which has been manufactured by men. For lack of bread and as a result of mal-distribution of bread, people starve and go hungry. It is this bread, bread tainted with human sin and selfishness and greed, which is offered at the Offertory. It brings with it the stain and injustice of the world from which it comes.[19]

It is precisely because of this 'worldliness' that the offering of bread and wine for the Supper can represent the offering of our lives. In the more ancient words of Augustine: 'There you are on the paten; there you are in the chalice.'

In more recent years, the liturgical tradition has reflected on such global situations as world debt, the economic domination of multi-national corporations, and other forms of unjust international monetary relationships. Mennonite John

Howard Yoder links these questions to the liturgical recitation of the Lord's Prayer. He argues that the word 'debts' in the Lord's Prayer is a word (*opheilema*) which is always used precisely to designate a *monetary* debt, and that the word 'forgive' (*apheimi*) implies a complete cancellation of that debt. This, he says, is what happens in the Old Testament Year of Jubilee: 'Jesus is not simply recommending vaguely that we might pardon those who have bothered us or made us trouble, but tells us purely and simply to erase the debts of those who owe us money; which is to say, practice the jubilee.'[20]

Sometimes the liturgy does its work in forming the assembly for the establishment of justice and peace in the world as much by what it *refrains* from saying as by what it says. For another contemporary exponent of the tradition, Lutheran Gordon Lathrop, the power of liturgical symbols lies in their ability to leave us longing for the fulfilment of God's reign. He speaks, for example, of the Lord's Supper as a 'hungry feast', 'where we receive only a sip of wine and a taste of bread, where we sing of the richness of God, but go away hungry; where we bind ourselves to the pain and hunger of the poor'.[21] We are presented in the liturgy with a vision of that Reign of God for which we hunger, indeed that Reign is present among us, and it is that which calls us forward to behave in particular ways. Roman Catholic Mark Searle argues:

> In [the Kingdom's] presence, we are confronted with that which we are called to be, with that which God would make us be, if we permit it. Thus, the liturgy not only provides us with a moral ideal but confronts us with an ontological reality in the light of which the ambivalence of our lives is revealed for what it is.[22]

In the end, our human quest for social justice is rooted in the liturgical proclamation of the lordship of Christ, 'the unique Liberator and the only Lord of history and of humankind'. As one Latin American liberation theologian expresses it:

> Thus it is proclaimed not simply that Christ is the only

Lord, but also that his lordship excludes all other dominions and lordships over humanity, and that in him we have become finally free. Socially speaking, it is proclaimed that we reject completely every kind of oppression that impedes human beings from achieving their destiny.[23]

Thus, the vision of, the presence of, and our longing for the kingdom of God manifested in the liturgy calls us to action. But the liturgy also allows us to see that the establishment of God's reign of justice and peace is not ultimately in our hands, since it is always a gift, springing ever new from the hand of God.

PRACTISING FORGIVENESS

We know very well that we are not unlucky, but evil.
W. H. Auden[24]

Accordingly, my dearest sons, hasten to the remedy of confession. Lay open your wounds in confession that the medicaments of healing may be able to take effect in you.
Alcuin[25]

As a part of our commitment to act responsibly is an equally important commitment to recognise when we have failed to act responsibly. We have seen that the liturgical tradition recognises the reality of sin and often looks upon the liturgy as a source of strength in the face of temptation. But in addition it provides the arena within which we seek forgiveness from God and from one another for what we have done amiss. To be willing to express repentance and to seek and accept forgiveness is not only indispensable to maintaining the health and well-being of the Christian community, but is also the prerequisite for all future ethical behaviour. Rowan Williams writes:

[T]o live a 'forgiven' life is not simply to live in a happy consciousness of having been absolved. Forgiveness is precisely the deep and abiding sense of what relation – with God or with other human beings – can and should be, and so it is itself a stimulus, an irritant, necessarily provoking protest at impoverished versions of social and personal relations.[26]

To be forgiven, then, as contemporary liturgist Christian Duquoc says, is not just a statement about one's spiritual condition at any particular moment. Forgiveness is always 'an invitation to the imagination'. It is not about 'forgetfulness of the past; but rather the risk of a future other than the one imposed by the past or memory'.[27] In asking and receiving a word of forgiveness we learn what it means to approach God 'without an alibi', and to learn the freedom that that brings:

> That is why I 'go to confession' regularly: to acknowledge my weakness and to celebrate the possibility of new beginnings. The sacrament of reconciliation helps me find and identify my longing and sets me on the road to the freedom for which I ache and from which I sometimes turn in dread. Freedom brings with it a terrible burden of responsibility. That is why we dread it. Freedom is the prerequisite for any kind of genuine loving. That is why we long for it.[28]

To experience forgiveness in and through the liturgy is to experience our own futures, and to open ourselves once again to God's offer of a future which is righteous.

The liturgy implicitly understands how and why people change: not by force, not by coercion, but by being presented with a vision of what we can be. In this way we are lifted beyond ourselves in order to discover new possibilities for faith and action. As theologian Jürgen Moltmann says, 'Where repentance is understood as a spiritual return to the evil and rejected past, it deals in self-accusation, contrition, sackcloth and ashes. But when repentance is a return to the future, it becomes concrete and rejoicing, in new self-confidence, and in love.'[29] In this way we can go forward courageously toward responsible action. Hearing the word of forgiveness, as Martin Luther says, 'fattens the bones and gives joy, security, and fearlessness to the conscience so that one dares all, can do all, and, in this trust in the grace of God, laughs even at death'.[30]

In addition to formal words of confession of sin and absolution, the liturgy embodies God's perpetual offer of forgiveness in a number of other concrete ways. In baptism, it is symbolised with the washing in water, which in the clear and consistent witness of the liturgical tradition, always represents renewed life. As Cyril of Jerusalem describes it:

> Why then is water [called] a spiritual grace? Because all things exist from water. It is water which gives life to green sprouts. Thunderstorms send water down from heaven. Water is everywhere the same, but is efficacious in many different ways... So the Holy Spirit, one, the same, undivided, dispenses grace to each as she wishes. Just as the dry tree, when it receives water begins to bud, so the sinful soul is deemed worthy of the Holy Spirit through repentance, brings forth clusters of righteousness.[31]

For this reason our baptism can be a continual source of spiritual reflection, and for many within the tradition to 'think on our baptism' is to renew our commitment to repent and to receive God's forgiveness. In the words of John Calvin: 'Therefore as often as we fall away, we ought to recall the memory of our baptism and fortify our mind with it, that we may be sure and confident of the forgiveness of sins.'[32]

In the same ways, the Lord's Supper becomes the periodic renewal of the promises God has made to us in our baptism. The Eucharist embodies the perpetual invitation to the table of forgiveness, where Christ stands with open arms to welcome us home. In a sermon on the spiritual value of the Supper, one fifth-century preacher refers back to Psalm 33:9, 'O Taste and see that the Lord is good!' and goes on to say:

> You tasted the fruit of disobedience, and you know that bitter is the food of the bitter counselor. Taste now the fruit of obedience which wards off peril, and know that it

is better and more profitable to obey God. You tasted out of due time, and you died. Eat in due time and you shall live. You chose to learn by trial the outcome of dis- obedience. Learn also by trial the benefits of obedience. 'Taste and see that I the Lord am good!'[33]

For the liturgical tradition of Christian spirituality, to eat of the Supper is to recall the sacrificial death of Jesus, and the new covenant of grace and forgiveness that continuously flows from the cross and resurrection. In so doing, we step again and again into what Richard Hooker called the 'circle of con- trition and joy'.

During the season of Lent, there is a particular emphasis on this circular process of repentance and reconciliation, and many within the liturgical tradition have highlighted the various ways in which the forty days deepen the commitment to godly living through sustained attention to the place of penitence in our redemption. One contemporary representa- tive of the tradition describes the process this way:

> The call to repentance is the invitation to take stock of our emotional programs for happiness based on institutional needs and to change them. This is the fundamental program of Lent. Year by year, as the spiritual journey evolves, the destructive influences of these underevalu- ated programs for happiness become more obvious and, in proportionate manner, the urgency to change these increases. Thus the process of conversion is initiated and carried on. The term of this process is the experience of inner resurrection celebrated in the Easter–Ascension mystery.[34]

At the end of the lenten journey is Holy Week, when the events which culminated in the crucifixion and resurrection of Jesus Christ are recalled, encouraging us to consider the ways in which we ourselves are complicit in all that seeks to destroy what is good and true. This is where we most clearly see the remarkable intersection between God's story and our story:

Holy Week culminates in a great conflict of love and trust that is played out in the heart of God. Holy Week is the Great Journey out of our private hells into the homecoming of new possibilities. Insofar as I am willing to enter into the mystery of this week, especially the Great Three Days at its end, I will learn what it is to love. Good Friday, Holy Saturday and Easter Day are all parts of one single event. They are expressions of God's love calling us home.[35]

In hearing once again the story of ultimate potency of God's love, in learning that it is 'as strong as death', we are encouraged to step forward once again and accept the invitation to love others, with all the risks and possibilities that this entails.

As we have seen, for the liturgical tradition the symbolic action in the liturgy is both expressive and empowering; it declares not only who we are, but contributes to forming us into who and what we will be. One of the most radical of these actions is the ritual of foot-washing which has been a part of the worship of a number of religious groups at various times in Christian history. It finds its origins in a scene described in the Fourth Gospel (John 13:1–20), in which Jesus washes the feet of his disciples and says to them, 'If I, your Lord and Teacher have washed your feet, you also ought to wash one another's feet.' And then later, 'I give you a new commandment, that you love one another. Just as I have loved you, you also should love one another. By this everyone will know that you are my disciples, if you have love for one another' (John 13: 34–35; NRSV).

Foot-washing has been particularly significant within the 'Believers' Churches', those Protestant denominations which have arisen out of the Radical Reformation of the sixteenth century. One contemporary Anabaptist describes an occasion during which the act of foot-washing was particularly significant in reconciliation within a community:

We began to see individuals whom we know had broken relationships, seeking one another out and washing their feet, we witnessed those who had struggled with each other for most of the year, embracing with tears in their eyes. Others would join them, making confession and seeking forgiveness... That evening I witnessed the broken body of Christ become so identified with the brokenness among us that God was able to resurrect new life through the healing and reconciling of relationships.[36]

The liturgical tradition is clear that this kind of reconciliation among members of the Christian community, good and healthy as it may be, is never an end in itself. It is only by being reconciled within itself that the Christian community can go on to act as an agent of reconciliation in the world at large.

TO IMAGINE THE WORLD 'AS IF'

The worship of God is not a rule of safety – it is an adventure of the spirit, a flight after the unattainable. The death of religion comes with the repression of the high hope of adventure.

Alfred North Whitehead[37]

Part of the liturgy's work is to invite people to envision the world in a different way, to imagine it as God intends it to be; indeed, to imagine the world 'as if' the reign of God has already been fully realised. For the liturgical tradition, this invitation to imagine happens in a number of ways in our corporate worship: in the sharing of bread and wine in the Lord's Supper without regard to rank or status; in the words of prayers of intercession for a violent world; in prayers of repentance for our own sin and words declaring God's amnesty; and in signs of reconciliation and peace among members of the congregation. Biblical scholar Walter Brueggemann describes this kind of exercise of the spiritual imagination as he reflects on the reading of Scripture within the liturgical assembly:

The action of meeting begins – music, word, prayer, theater. At its center, the minister reads (or has read) these very old words, remote, archaic, something of a threat, something of yearning. In the listening, one hears another world proposed. It is an odd world of 'no male or female,' of condemned harlots and welcomed women, of sheep and goats judged, of wheat and tares tolerated, of heavy commandments and free grace, of food given only for work, and widows and orphans valued in their nonproductivity. If one listens long and hard, what emerges is a different world.[38]

In other words, the images and actions of the liturgy present a fundamental challenge to the status quo; they invite us to encounter the world not as passive observers, but as those who are seeking the mystery of God's presence within the processes of time and history.

In addition to giving us a window onto God's relationship with human history, the liturgy also gives us, in various ways, a foretaste of the ultimate destiny of material creation as a whole. In what is often called the 'economics of the liturgy,' bread, wine, water, fire, oil and physical space are not exploited and manipulated for short-term and selfish ends (as they so often are in our common experience), but find their place as bearers of divine presence, which is the destiny of all creation. In the view of many in the liturgical tradition of Christian spirituality, this is what the Church intends to signify by pronouncing words of blessing over things. In the words of the *Constitution on the Liturgy*: 'When the Church blesses, the world is given a transparency regarding its origin and its end.'[39]

But the liturgical tradition is always quick to warn us against self-absorption or self-satisfaction. Indeed, the liturgy drives us away from this kind of moral complacency. Merle Strenge, an Anabaptist, writes:

> To the extent that we practice the politics of remembering, we will become a people less likely to wait for John Wayne and the cavalry to ride to our rescue by employing the violent weapons of the world. Instead, like Elisha, we will be enabled to see the armies of the Lord ranging on the

hills surrounding those who would destroy us, armies of a Lord who will instruct us not to kill our enemies but invite them to a banquet before sending them home in peace (II Kings 8:23).[40]

Many within the liturgical tradition of spirituality echo Strenge's sentiments, and view the images and symbols of the liturgy as essentially disturbing, *intended* to cause us spiritual discomfort, intended to be a goad to the Christian conscience.

Although most closely associated with the Orthodox traditions of worship, the notion that in the liturgy we receive a 'foretaste of heaven' is found in nearly all those who have thought about the meaning and purpose of common prayer.[41] Anglican theologian Norman Pittenger says that as we stand before God in our worship we 'stand for the moment "in heaven"':

> That is our God-intended destiny. As we are fed with the life of God in Christ, we 'eat the bread which came down from heaven.' That is our God-given strengthening. The liturgy then leads us out into the world, where we must act as Christians precisely because it does not let us rest content with the world *as it is*, but drives us to acknowledge that we are here as 'resident aliens,' with a tremendous task imposed upon us. We are to make over that colony in which we dwell until it becomes in truth a 'colony of heaven,' even while our hearts can never forget and must often yearn for the homeland.[42]

Many reach back into the Christian liturgy's Jewish past for further insight into this relationship between the now of the liturgical life and the not yet of God's future. An example of this is the keeping of Sabbath. Jewish liturgist Lawrence Hoffmann writes:

> They [kept the Sabbath] as a sign of what was to come, an end to want, the mending of divisiveness, a universe repaired to its own integral harmony ... Shabbat, then, was more than a day of rest, more than a day merely to

refrain from work. It was a cosmic glimpse into eternity, the promise of incalculable joy at the end of time, a certain sign of fragmentation's end, life's wholeness before our very eyes.[43]

The liturgical tradition is clear that within the liturgical assembly we can set our quest for moral and responsible lives within the wider context of God's eternal purposes for the world. As Aidan Kavanagh argues:

> Because of its eschatological intent, liturgy is about nothing less than ultimate, rather than immediate, survival. It is about life forever by grace and promise. Liturgy regards anything less as a trap and a delusion, hostile to the gospel of Jesus Christ . . . [L]ike the Sabbath, liturgy is for us in that it summons us by revealed Good News home to a Presence, to a life even now of communion in that Presence. To commune with that Presence is to be in at the end and at the center where the world is whole, fresh, and always issuing new from the Father's hand through Christ in the Spirit.[44]

A spirituality which issues from faithful participation in the liturgy, then, will never be content to rest in the status quo. At the very least, the abundance of the liturgical symbols of God's generosity towards us reveals to us the impoverishment all around us.

6. NEGOTIATING SICKNESS, DYING AND DEATH

Sickness, dying and death: for us, as for generations of faithful people before us, the facts of human mortality present potent challenges to our relationship with God. What does our human frailty say about the God who has created and redeemed us? How are we to respond to our own suffering and to the suffering of others, and how do we expect God to respond? On what do we rest our hope, finally and fully? These are questions with which all traditions of Christian spirituality must wrestle. Those within the liturgical tradition of Christian spirituality do not claim to have arrived at any startlingly original answers to these questions; but they are convinced that because common prayer is rooted in and expresses the whole range of human experience (including human morbidity and death), it provides a singular opportunity for godly insight. Within the rites of baptism, healing, the Lord's Supper, penance, the Church year, and Christian burial lies a treasury of images and patterns of devotional experience which allow not only for serious reflection upon our human mortality, but also for incorporating that reflection into the overall fabric of our spiritual lives.

THE PROBLEM OF SICKNESS

Illness is the night side of life, a more onerous citizenship. Everyone who is born holds dual citizenship, in the kingdom of the well and the kingdom of the sick. Although we all prefer to use only the good passport, sooner or

later each of us is obliged, at least for a spell, to identify
ourselves as citizens of that other place.

Simone Weil

When we fall ill, we not only experience pain and debility, but
many of our most essential relationships are also profoundly
altered. As those involved in the pastoral care of the sick have
often observed, physical infirmity has the capacity to dislocate
and disconnect us in various aspects of our lives, mental,
physical, social and spiritual. One commentator observes:

> In illness the human person experiences a multiple
> estrangement, from one's own body, from friends and
> associates, from the doings of society, and from God. Sin,
> as a global reality rather than simply as personal offense,
> has a hold on the person through this alienation. The
> spirit is weakened by the bodily condition and conversely
> weakness of spirit makes the effort to deal with the bodily
> condition difficult.[1]

In addition, as Susan Sontag points out,[2] our difficulties with
being ill arise not only from the sickness itself, from its pain
and from its ability to disconnect us from others, but also from
the various metaphors, images and stereotypes by which our
society interprets illness. Illness is looked upon as an enemy
to be defeated, an abnormal deformity of 'real life', a deviant
state, and to the extent that we internalise these images we
look upon *ourselves* as abnormal, deviant and in collusion with
the forces of evil.

Sickness may also occasion serious spiritual difficulties for
those who form the community of the sick or suffering person:
relatives and friends, neighbours, care-givers and fellow
Christians. Sometimes these difficulties result from a sense
that we are unable to do for the infirm what we know we
should be doing, and often simply by the range of emotions
and responses that the sickness itself brings out in us. Our
fears of contagion, our feelings of impotence or impatience in
the face of pain, our desire to deny our own mortality can

create a spiritual crisis for us as well. As Simone Weil observes, 'The capacity to give one's attention to a sufferer is a very rare and difficult thing; it is almost a miracle; it is a miracle.'[3] If we are not up to this difficult, 'almost-a-miracle' task, we may feel as if our own relationship with God is in jeopardy.

For the liturgical tradition of spirituality, Christian worship provides an invaluable resource not only for appropriating sickness and health into the complex web of our spiritual lives, but also for providing alternative metaphors by which to understand illness, and models by which to learn to respond to it. Pre-eminent in this task are the rites of healing. Healing within the Christian community is a very ancient practice, rooted in and patterned on the healing ministry of Jesus. We see it already well established in the injunctions in the New Testament Letter of James, where the link between human sickness and human sin is also made:

> Are any among you sick? They should call the elders of the church and have them pray over them, anointing them with oil in the name of the Lord. The prayer of faith will save the sick, and the Lord will raise them up; and anyone who has committed sins will be forgiven. (James 4:13–15; NRSV)

Of course Christians are not alone in recognising the value of ritual in the reinterpretation and reintegration of sickness into our quest for holiness. As a contemporary commentator says:

> [Sickness] is one of those privileged intervals which societies have surrounded with ritual intended to enable the individual and the group to negotiate the sometimes treacherous corridor that stretches between the moment of separation from the familiar and that of entry into the world of the new. Whether for the sick that be a world constituted by recovery, chronic illness, or by death, they themselves enter it and are transformed by what has taken place in the passage, shaped by its rites.[4]

The deep human need to infuse the experience of sickness with meaning is shared, and finds its expression today even among highly secularised people, and in settings which are not explicitly religious, such as hospitals and hospices. According to some observers, whenever we send flowers to the sick, whenever surgeons dress and scrub for surgery, whenever nurses perform the ritual routines of the hospital, they are participating in the 'rites of passage' of human sickness, allowing for the creation of meaning by giving patient, care-taker, and observer a greater sense of control over the mysterious processes of disease.

However, those within the liturgical tradition of spirituality ask us to focus on the way in which healing rituals within the Church enable people to find explicitly Christian meaning in the experience of sickness, whether it is their own sickness or the sickness of others. By setting the rites of healing within the Christian community (which is itself called to be a community of healing and reconciliation), and by linking them not only to Jesus' own healing but to the healing implicit in his resurrection, the healing rituals of Christianity evoke powerful images which allow both the sick and those around them to forge meaning out of a potentially meaningless situation. The rites of healing allow the sick person to enter into and to 'live the mystery [of Christ's dying and rising] in sickness and to live this condition, rather than simply endure it, and share in this mystery'.[5] In this way sick persons are 'enabled to be witnesses in the community, to faith and to hope and to the deeper qualities of the human'.[6]

The traditional, ritual lynch-pin of the rites of healing is the laying-on-of-hands, often accompanied by anointing with oil. Both of these gestures have long been associated with the indwelling of the Holy Spirit within the sick person, expressing symbolically the power of the Spirit, not only as the provider of healing and comfort, but also as the essential bond between all Christians, a bond established at baptism and remaining steadfast even after death. The medieval Sarum Missal speaks of the oil of healing as 'a heavenly medicine, a spiritual remedy, an inward and abiding unction, unto the strengthening and healing of the soul and mind and body, and the renewal of the indwelling of the Holy Ghost in thy living temple'.[7] Or, as a more contemporary representative of the liturgical tradition says, in the anointing and laying-on-of-hands, 'those who feel abandoned by God or their brothers and sisters' through sickness 'discover the Paraclete, the Comforter, at the same moment they discover the warmth of human touch in the laying on of hands'.[8]

But what does the liturgical tradition of Christian spirituality say about the event of healing itself? Is the healing ritual intended to heal, to cure the person of his or her illness, or is it simply to provide the occasion for finding meaning, comfort and a sense of control in the midst of sickness? For some Christian traditions, the anointing of the sick with the laying-on-of-hands is looked upon as a 'sacrament' of the Church. This means it is understood as having effective power. 'A sacrament is not just an empty sign, an aesthetic symbol,' one representative of the liturgical tradition states, 'it contains and requires what it signifies.'[9] How is this sacramental power 'effective' in the case of human sickness?

In answer to this question, most within the liturgical tradition would say that the creation of meaning which the rites of healing enable is itself a form of healing. The Orthodox liturgist Alexander Schmemann warns us not to think of a sacrament as some sort of 'miracle':

> by which God breaks, so to speak, the 'laws of nature,' but [rather as] the manifestation of the ultimate Truth about the world and life, man and nature, the Truth which is Christ. And healing is a sacrament because its purpose or end is not *health* as such, the restoration of physical health, but the entrance of man into the 'joy and peace' of the Holy Spirit. In Christ, everything in this world, and this means health and disease, joy and suffering, has become an ascension to, an entrance into this new life, its expectation and anticipation.[10]

For the liturgical tradition of spirituality, then, the 'effect' of the Christian healing rites lies, first and foremost, in their ability to 'reframe' the sickness, to place it within the context of God's ultimate purposes for us, to provide comfort and an experience of Christian society for the sick person (which is an embodiment and a foretaste of the comfort and society promised to those who live by faith). A clear distinction is being made here between 'curing' and 'healing', between the elimination of disease and the incorporation of disease into the complexity of human experience and especially into the resurrection life in which Christians are called to participate by virtue of their baptism. Sometimes the curing of disease does indeed take place, through the sacrament of anointing, through the liturgy of the Lords Supper, by allowing the church year and Daily Office to be vehicles of the healing power of God. Curing also happens through the ministrations of medical and surgical personnel, through the care and concern of friends and relatives, by means of remedial treatments of various kinds. But even in these cases, it is the liturgy which allows us to see that the physical cure, whatever its immediate cause, is ultimately a gift of God.

In addition, the liturgy enables us to put human health in a wider perspective. Healing, either in the sense of the curing of disease or in the sense of the healing of the soul, is *for* something, for something more than just the well-being of the sick person, as important as that may be. The wider meaning of physical and spiritual healing varies according to the particular strand of the liturgical tradition of spirituality we choose to pick up. For many of the earliest representatives of this tradition, the healing rites (and the human healing they signify and effect) are proof of the resurrection of Jesus and of our participation in the resurrection promises of God. In the words of Ireneus of Lyons:

> For what was [God's] object in healing members of the flesh, and restoring them to their pristine condition, if they, having been healed by him, were not to obtain

salvation? ... Whoever, therefore, confers healing, confers life; and whoever gives life, also wraps his handwork in incorruption.[11]

Like the raising of Lazarus (John 11:1–44), any healing is a foretaste of eternal life; but this is not simply a 'pie-in-the-sky-by-and-by-when-we-die' form of spiritual assurance. We are to model and to reveal our participation in this reality, as individuals and as a Christian community, in every aspect of our lives:

> [The rite of] healing can provide no guarantee against death, but it sets one free from the desperate feeling that one is living only to die, and allows one to opt for life even in death. Recovery and liberation thus become synonymous. To be healed is to begin to become capable of accepting, sharing, making the most of concrete possibilities of human existence, in anticipation of that fullness of humanity to which we are all called in Christ.[12]

A spirituality that looks to the liturgy for guidance sets forth a vision of a liberated life, a life free to love, give, create, rejoice and hope, even in the midst of sickness, even in the midst of suffering and in the face of death. In a very real sense, then, the rites of healing proclaim that we are healed, in body, mind and spirit, in order that we might fully participate in the progressive establishment of a future in which all things will ultimately be healed and brought into holy relationship with God and with other creatures.

OTHER FORMS OF CHRISTIAN WORSHIP AND HUMAN HEALTH

If the rites of healing forge the most obvious link between sickness, spirituality and liturgy, perhaps an even more ancient connection is made between the understanding of sickness and participation in the Eucharist. The witness of the liturgical tradition is clear and consistent: to receive com-

munion in faith is to receive the healing presence of Jesus
Christ, to be infused with the power of the Holy Spirit, the
Comforter, and to be radically oriented toward our ultimate
destiny. Clement of Alexandria, for example, wishes us to
regard the Lord's Supper as the 'food of incorruptability'.
Quoting John's Gospel (6:51), Clement remarks:

> Since, [Jesus] said 'the bread which I will give is my flesh'
> and because as well, blood flows through the flesh, and
> because wine, taken allegorically, means blood, it must
> be understood thus: when morsels of bread are added to
> adulterated wine the bread absorbs the wine and leaves
> only that which is watery. In the same way the flesh of
> the Lord, the bread of heaven, absorbs the blood [of human
> persons] raising those who are heavenly to incorrupt-
> ability, and leave only the carnal desires destined for
> corruption.[13]

The Supper feeds us with the reality of our future state, and
in so doing provides a 'balm for the soul', a soul which is being
assaulted by the pain and suffering, the dehumanisation and
the social isolation of illness.

Many spiritual biographies and autobiographies attest to
the restorative power of the Lord's Supper in the face of human
weakness. There is the poignant description of the tenth-
century Saint Melania, who was lying gravely ill in her cell in
the monastery at Jerusalem, unable to take her usual place
assisting at Holy Communion. Her friend and confessor Geron-
tius was saying Mass in the next room, but was so affected by
grief at the seriousness of Melania's condition that he was
rendered unable to recite the eucharistic prayers aloud. Suddenly the voice of Melania could be heard through the partition
which separated her room from the convent chapel. 'Pronounce
the prayers in a louder voice, please,' Melania was heard to
say, 'that I may hear them and be strengthened by their
power.'[14] These were her last words. She knew what an earlier
representative of this spiritual tradition, Ignatius of Antioch,
knew, that even at the point of death the Eucharist functions

as 'spiritual therapy'. Ignatius calls it the 'medicine of immortality, an antidote which results not in dying but in living forever in Jesus Christ'.[15]

The liturgical tradition also finds significant resources for uncovering the spiritual meaning in the experience of human weakness in the keeping of the Christian year, particularly in our common worship during Holy Week, which speaks in various ways of pain and weakness. We recall the humility and betrayal woven into Jesus' last Passover meal on Maundy Thursday; we hear the poignant words in the Garden of Gethsemane ('My Father, if it is possible, let this cup pass from me; yet not what I want, but what you want' [Matthew 26:39b]); we allow ourselves to stand at the foot of the cross on Good Friday, and to meditate on the agony of execution. The repetition of these experiences year after year, the progressive internalising of these images and narratives, allows worshippers gradually to enter into what the liturgy calls 'the mystery of faith'; to see that redemption is found precisely at the meeting-point between God and human suffering.[16] For those who must somehow integrate their own debility into the tapestry of their spirituality, the Christian liturgical calendar can be a unique and invaluable resource.

Two further liturgical resources are important as primary resources for integrating sickness and infirmity into the totality of our relationship with God. Within the liturgical tradition of spirituality both the Daily Office and the penitential rites (also called Reconciliation), allow us to express, verbally and ritually, the diverse and often ambiguous responses to illness. In various ways both the Office and Reconciliation allow the sick a way of being radically honest, in the presence of God and other Christians, an honesty which is seen to encourage the health and well-being of body, mind and spirit. In many traditions, the Daily Office is the occasion for proceeding systematically through all one hundred and fifty psalms, carrying the worshipper through the full range of human emotions, and opening up the possibility of bringing before God even those feelings which are most covert and distressing. 'We can be grateful', Roman Catholic liturgist Nathan Mitchell observes, 'that the psalms . . . do not flinch at misery and pain. Shamelessly, they rant, snarl, bark, bite, kick, scream, pinch and pull hair.'[17] In so doing, they allow us to be truthful before God as we confront the reality of human sickness.

Throughout the history of Christianity, the connection between human sickness and human sinfulness is a complex and ambiguous one. As the earliest Christian communities reflected on the healing miracles of Jesus, the question about the origins of sickness immediately arose ('Who sinned, this man or his father?'[18] 'For which is easier to say, "Your sins are forgiven," or to say, "Stand up and walk"?'[19]), and even though no clear answer has emerged, the Church's ancient and enduring insistence that rituals for the confession of sin and assurance of pardon should be integrated within the rites for anointing of the sick attests to a reciprocal relationship between the human estrangement from God and illness. More recently, the effects of guilt and shame on human health have been widely studied, and many contemporary exponents of the liturgical tradition have used arguments from the human sciences to bolster their arguments for the spiritual and physical benefits of rituals for the confession of sin.

Healing rites, forms of reconciliation, the Eucharist, the church year: the liturgical tradition of Christian spirituality often looks to these various individual rites and patterns of worship which make up the complex reality that is the liturgical life of the Church as it asks questions about the spiritual meaning of human infirmity. But it must be said that the more pervasive testimony of the tradition is that the liturgy as a whole, as the on-going renewal of our relationship with the sacrificial living, suffering, death and resurrection of Jesus Christ, is the overarching context within which Christians integrate sickness into the spiritual life. As one contemporary exponent of the tradition says, 'It is indeed fundamental to reflect on the relation of human suffering and sickness to the paschal mystery of Christ and to ask what promise Christ's death and resurrection holds out to the ill.'[20] This is not so much about particular graces and benefits of specific sacramental activities, but about the corporate worship of the Church as the 'environment' within which people are enabled to come to a renewed understanding of sickness as a part of their own self-identity, and as part of their relationship with their fellow human beings and with God.

A LITURGICAL SPIRITUALITY OF DYING AND DEATH

> Just as Jesus perfected the water of baptism, so too he drew off death; for this reason we go down into the water, so that we are not poured out into the wind of the world. Whenever the latter blows, winter comes; whenever the Holy Spirit blows, summer comes.
>
> *The Gospel According to Philip*

If sickness is a serious challenge to the stability and well-being of our spiritual life, then dying and death is perhaps the ultimate challenge. We trust that where Jesus has gone, we shall follow, through death and despair to resurrection life. But the reality of our own death and the death of those we love puts that trust to the test. The process of making sense of death is complicated for twenty-first-century people by the fact of living in the midst of a death-denying culture,[21] in which the dying are routinely removed from the living and placed in clinical settings, and in which to think and speak of death is considered 'morbid' or 'macabre'. Where can we turn for help as we attempt to claim the assurance that ultimately we are not simply 'poured out into the wind of the world'?

For those in the liturgical tradition of spirituality, the 'school of prayer' which is the liturgy teaches us the meaning of our death, gives us the words, images, and rituals by which to speak honestly about death and dying, and provides us with the tools to undertake the task of 'dying well'. But the liturgy not only speaks to us of our own death and the death of those we love. It also invites us to confront the meaning of death as a profound human reality, a reality woven into the fabric of the world and its history. Theologian Karl Rahner describes what happens when a person truly enters into the spirit of the liturgy, into what he calls the recapitulation of 'the whole colossal history of birth and death' which was assumed and redeemed by Jesus Christ in his life, death and resurrection. Such a person

> is profoundly aware of the drama into which his life is unceasingly drawn, the drama of the world, the divine Tragedy and the divine Comedy. He thinks of the dying, those facing their end glassy eyed with the death rattle in their throat, and he knows that this fate has taken up lodging in his own being. He feels in himself the groaning of the creature and the world, their demand for a more hopeful future . . . He bears within himself something of the laughter of children in their unshadowed, future-laden joy; within him resounds also the weeping of the starving children, the agony of the sick, the bitterness caused by betrayed love.[22]

What Rahner is pointing to is the deep interpenetration between what he calls 'the liturgy of the world' and 'the liturgy of the Church'. As liturgist Mark Searle says, 'the liturgy of Christ's life and death is the culmination of that liturgy [of the world], and it is that liturgy and its redemptive culmination that we celebrate in the liturgy of the Church'.

THE LITURGY AND THE CROWN OF MARTYRDOM

Very early in the Church's history we see the insights of the liturgical tradition of Christian spirituality taking shape in this matter of dying and death, and among those who can almost universally be reckoned as representatives of this tradition are the Christians who died under persecution confessing their faith in Christ. As the principal 'school of prayer' for the dying, the prayers, images and rituals of the

Christian liturgy were almost invariably used to express the meaning of the martyrs' death at the point of their death. As one modern commentator observes:

> the words that came spontaneously to their lips were often the same expressions they were accustomed to using in the liturgical gatherings. The gestures with which they took leave of their brethren while they awaited the palm of martyrdom were the same ritual gestures they were accustomed to repeating in the synaxis.[23]

And so we find Polycarp, for example, sentenced to death sometime in the early years of the second century, offering a thanksgiving prayer clearly patterned after the Great Thanksgiving over the bread and wine of the Eucharist, in which he 'blesses' God for considering him worthy of a martyr's death, through which he is privileged to receive a 'portion' from the 'cup of your Christ'.

When we look at chroniclers' descriptions of the last moments of those being put to death for their faith, we see over and over again that the Church's common prayer is used as the principal interpretive resource. When the time for death came, the condemned would exchange the kiss of peace with other members of the Christian community, as they would ordinarily do in the worship service before partaking of the Lord's Supper; and when the lion sprang, the swordsman lunged, or the fire was lit, the martyr almost invariably raised his or her hands into the 'orans' position, arms extended over the head, palms facing outward, the traditional position for liturgical prayer. When Polycarp was burned at the stake for his faith, his biographer describes the look and smell of his burning flesh as 'like bread in the baking', a clear reference to the principal liturgical symbol of human sacrifice unto death, the eucharistic bread. Likewise Ignatius, writing to the Christian community in Rome on his way to martyrdom, finds in the liturgy poignant and powerful metaphors for his impending death: 'This favor I beg you,' he writes, 'Suffer me to be a libation poured out to God, while there is still an altar

waiting for me ... I am his wheat, ground fine by the lions'
teeth to make purest bread for Christ.'

In addition, the martyr's arrival in heaven is often portrayed
as the arrival at the heavenly liturgy. In the account of the
martyrdom of Perpetua and Felicity (203), we hear the words
of the saints describing their entry into the presence of God:

> And we entered and, we heard a voice saying, 'Holy, holy,
> holy' without ceasing ... And the other elders said to us,
> 'Let us stand.' And we stood and gave the kiss of peace.
> And the elders said, 'Go and play.' And I said to Perpetua,
> 'You have your wish.' And she said to me, 'Thanks be to
> God, that as I was merry in the flesh, so am I now still
> merrier here.'[24]

What we see in all of these accounts is an approach to death
that can only be described as 'joyful'. And again, it is from the
liturgy that this spirit of joy is gleaned. Even the funeral and
burial rites in the early Church were occasions not for sadness,
but for the celebration of what was referred to as the Christian's 'heavenly birthday', for the singing of hymns of
thanksgiving to God, for the wearing of white garments reminiscent of those which were put on new Christians at their
baptism.

CHRISTIAN BAPTISM AND CHRISTIAN DEATH

> Do you not know that all of us who have been baptized
> into Christ Jesus were baptized into his death? Therefore
> we have been buried with him by baptism into death, so
> that, just as Christ was raised from the dead by the glory
> of the Father, so we too might walk in newness of life.
>
> (Romans 6:3–4)

From the time of the earliest Christian communities, the rites
of Christian initiation have been infused with images of death.
Baptism is understood as a symbolic plunging into the death
and resurrection of Christ, as an infusion of the power of the

Holy Spirit for participation in the mission God to overcome the forces of death in the world, and as the inauguration of a form of life that survives even death. In an ancient homily, Theodore of Mopsuestia, speaks to those who have been baptised at Easter about the relationship between the reality of their baptism and the reality of their death:

> It is in that faith [that Christ has done away with death] that we approach and are baptized, because we wish to share in his death, in hope of sharing in those same good things, namely to rise from the dead in the manner that he has risen. For that reason, when I am baptized, by immersing my head, it is the death of our Lord Jesus Christ which I receive, and his burial which I wish to take upon myself; and there truly, I already confess the resurrection of our Lord whilst in raising my head as a kind of figure, I perceive myself to be already raised.[25]

As the psalmist reminds us, the dead cannot praise God. And Christians have always believed that in baptism we begin the song of praise to God which will last throughout eternity.

The liturgical tradition neither minimises nor avoids the reality of human death and dying. In baptism Christians have traditionally been marked on the forehead with the sign of the cross, the sign of new life which comes precisely in and through the sacrificial death of Jesus; on Ash Wednesday, 'in a dramatic and powerful annual repetition of baptism, [we are marked] with an ashen cross':

> Young and old, aged and infants, all have the cross that was engraved on their foreheads when they were baptized solemnly redrawn with ashes accompanied with the sobering reminder, 'You are dust, and to dust you shall return.' The water of life is suspended, and the desiccated remainder, ashes, speaks of inevitable death and decay in all that is cut off from God. And yet, ashes are an ancient cleansing agent, and, learning again our mortality, we are cleansed of pride and illusion and enabled to see ourselves

as we truly are. The clarification begins on Ash Wednesday with a cross drawn with ashes, and it culminates in the renewal of baptismal vows and sprinkling with Easter water at the Great Vigil. We move from dust to water, from a dead end to hope, from the grave to life.[26]

The liturgy of Ash Wednesday, recapitulating the liturgy of baptism, tells us clearly that we are dust and destined to return to dust; but the liturgy also tells us that we are more than dust and destined for more than a return to dust.

In all of these things, we look forward to the moment of our death, when we will discover if those things we have rehearsed in the liturgy have truly transformed us and in transforming us have prepared us for the process of dying. We have sung with the psalmist, 'Do not let the flood sweep over me, or the deep swallow me up, or the Pit close its mouth over me' (Psalm 69:15); we know that we are deserving of death and yet we have heard, year in and year out, the promises of resurrection. The liturgical tradition of spirituality looks upon all of this as a process which beckons us toward a meaningful dying. Using the imagery of baptism, Martin Luther reminds us:

> Those who are baptized are condemned to die, and there-fore the whole of life is nothing else than a spiritual baptism which does not cease till death. Therefore the life of a Christian, from beginning to the grave, is nothing else than the beginning of a blessed death.[27]

THE LORD'S SUPPER AS THE 'MEDICINE OF IMMORTALITY'

> But where the Lord's church, the dear disciples of Christ, have met in Christ's name to partake of the Holy Supper in true faith, love, and obedience, there the outward per-ishable man eats and drinks perishable bread and wine, and the inner imperishable man of the heart eats in a spiritual sense the imperishable body and blood of Christ

which cannot be eaten or digested . . . Like is benefited by like.

Menno Simons[28]

Those within this tradition of Christian spirituality find in the imagery of the Lord's Supper exceptionally potent metaphors for understanding the true nature of human dying and death. Our bodies are likened to wheat that is ground up in death to make fine bread-flour, our life is poured out like wine; we are not, however, ground up and poured out for nothing, but, like the eucharistic elements, for participation in the life-giving activity of God. Just as the inner reality of the eucharistic bread is imperishable, contrary to appearances, so too is our own inner reality imperishable, despite the appearance of bodily death and decay. One early exponent of the tradition, Ireneus of Lyons, puts it this way:

> Our thinking [in the matter of the resurrection of the body] is consonant with the Eucharist, and the Eucharist in turn confirms our thinking . . . For just as bread which is produced from the earth, receiving the invocation of God is no longer ordinary bread, but the Eucharist, consisting of two elements, earthly and heavenly, so our bodies, receiving the Eucharist, are no longer corruptible, having the hope of resurrection.[29]

In addition, as we have seen, since the Lord's Supper provides an imperishable bond between and among Christians, the vision of the 'Heavenly Banquet' becomes the principal metaphor for life after death in the liturgical tradition of spirituality. The boundary between life and death, between the community of the living on earth and the community of those who have died, is dissolved in the liturgy of the Table. In one particularly moving poem from the eighteenth century, this sense of timeless communion is expressed:

> Show the people round the table
> Outspread, white as mountain sleet,
> Gather, the blue heavens above them,

And their dead beneath their feet;
There in perfect reconcealment
Death and life immortal meet
Noiseless round that fair white table
'Mid their fathers' tombstones spread
Hoary-headed elders moving
Bear the hallowed wine and bread,
While devoutly still the people
Low in prayer bow the head.[30]

But it is not sufficient to say that for the liturgical tradition of spirituality the Eucharist simply provides us with images and metaphors for understanding the meaning of death. For most within the tradition, partaking of the Lord's Supper in faith is an *effectual* partaking in the risen life of the Lord, drawing us out of the grip of death and into the realm of eternal life.

It is this sense of spiritual potency inherent in the celebration of the Eucharist that allowed John Chrysostom to speak of it as the 'medicine of immortality'. For much of the history of the Church it was the custom that the last act of the dying person was to receive communion, called the 'viaticum' – meaning 'that which goes with you on your way'. As one medieval commentator says, 'Indeed because a long way and a steep ascent still lies before anyone making such a difficult and arduous climb, this food is of the greatest necessity along the way that you walk – whence its name, as it is called, "the viaticum." '[31] At the same time, those within the liturgical tradition of Christian spirituality have seen the Supper as the embodiment of the promise of God not to hold our sins against us for all eternity, the embodiment of the persistent offer of forgiveness and mercy. 'You cannot at the same time eat at the table of the Lord and the table of demons', Saint Paul reminds the Roman Christians. At the point of death, we are nourished on the Good News of God's mercy, which we carry with us on the journey into the borderlands of our existence.

All of this has serious implications for the process of dying, and for finding and making meaning within it. If the Lord's Supper is both a fund of metaphors and images from which to draw, and at the same time an efficacious source of strength and sustenance, a sharing in the resurrection life of Jesus and in his promises to be with us in life and in death, then having found for ourselves a form of eucharistic spirituality for living, we should be able to activate that very same eucharistic spirituality for dying.

> For those, however, who have entered into the Eucharistic dimension [of life] by constant thanksgiving and mutual appreciation, and in a living faith, the whole life-experience is different. And when death approaches they can, with St. Francis, greet it as a beloved sister, as the gracious coming of the Lord, the final homecoming. For them, death will never just mean the last and final loss, the summit of senselessness, the helpless rebellion, but rather the hour of final transfiguration, of trust and peace.[32]

CHRISTIAN BURIAL AND CHRISTIAN HOPE

It has long been noted by those who provide pastoral care to grieving families that the Christian funeral has a significant role to play. As a way of proclaiming the resurrection hope, as a way of expressing the ambiguous emotions often occasioned by death, as a way commending the dead to the mercy of God and of re-incorporating the bereaved into the Christian community, the images, words, gestures and symbols of the burial liturgy are indispensable. One student of Christian ritual says:

> The funeral sets our personal senselessness within the context of wider sense, easing our intolerable feelings of frustrated impotence when our interior world is shattered by something beyond our control – a blow we cannot sustain, a mental and emotional chaos we cannot contain ... The funeral uses the shape of the rite of passage in order to give our thoughts and feelings the

direction, and consequently the significance, that they so desperately need for the shape of the passage rite is specially contrived to express and contain – to embody – the chaos involved in all genuine change that takes place at an existential level.[33]

To bring the complex web of feelings, especially the negative feelings, before God and our community in the burial rite has more than just psychological benefits, as important as these might be. The liturgical tradition is clear about the spiritual benefits, the benefits to our search for godly living in the face of the pain, remorse and resentment that are inevitable parts of life. Despite the overarching sense of joy at the death of a member of the Body of Christ, the psalms of lament have also traditionally found a place in the Christian funeral. As one contemporary representative of the tradition says:

> Lament needs to be an integral part of Christian practice in response to death and dying, precisely because we value so highly God's gift of earthly life . . . Death is an irrevocable, wrenching loss for those the dead leave behind. But it is also a loss for those who die – a loss of the parts of creation they took delight in, in the relationships they held most dear, and the possibilities they envisioned for the future . . . Hope of everlasting life with God does not undercut Christian gratitude and concern for this life, nor deny the place of lament in Christian responses to death.[34]

To assert the hope of resurrection in the face of death, in the face of grief and loss, is perhaps the bravest thing Christians are ever called upon to do. Much of this takes place not in the form of the words that are said, but in the rituals and symbols that are employed: the Paschal candle, standing by the coffin as it did by the font at our baptism; the pouring of dirt into the grave, with the words of the Ash Wednesday service echoing in our ears, 'Ashes to ashes, dust to dust'; the kiss of peace shared among those who remain, given and received in the knowledge that the deceased remain within the bonds of Christian love; the ancient practice of the crowning of the dead, still practised in some branches of the Orthodox Church, and affirming the conviction that in death we share fully in the life of Christ, prophet, priest and king.

> The symbolism of religious ritual embraces more than the circumscribed needs of the individual . . . Symbolism is a kind of expanded thought capable of bearing an emotional load that would otherwise remain inexpressible precisely because it is unthinkable. The symbol enables us to come to terms on an intuitive level with facts whose literal meaning we cannot yet deal with.[35]

As important as ritual may be in situations of profound grief, the words of the burial rites are not insignificant. Spiritual autobiographies in every century are filled with descriptions of the multiple ways in which the words spoken in the Christian worship occasioned by the death of a Christian convey spiritual strength and insight to those who are bereaved. Widows speak of the power of singing the same hymn at their husband's funeral which was sung at their wedding; when a young child has died, parents often speak of being given new hope in hearing the words from the baptismal rite; stories shared aloud give friends a way of expressing their thanksgiving to God for having shared in this particular life that has been lost in death. And above all, the proclamation of the resurrection hope in the words of Scripture, in a place where the dead worshipped, as it is each Sunday of the year, gives to worshippers a deep sense of the underlying 'holy stability' which is often masked by the uncertainties of life. It is always important to remember that those who speak of the power of the liturgy in this way, ordinary men, women and children, are just as true representatives of the liturgical tradition of Christian spirituality as those who are more well known and widely known.

THE CHRISTIAN VOCATION OF THE DYING

'It might just be one of God's surprises for us,' says Maggie
Kuhn, leader of the activist group the Gray Panthers, 'that he
may use those closest to death – nearer to the other life – to
show the Church how to break with self-centered purposes
and goals and look to the good of all and serve that good.'[36]
This is the challenge which has confronted us in every age,
but is particularly acute in the present age of high technology,
in which the unprecedented power over life and death makes
the dying increasingly passive recipients of biotechnical inter-
ventions. Can we learn to see a dying person not simply as
the 'object' of the ministry of others, but as having an active
role in the mission of God, a unique and irreplaceable ministry,
which is only completed at death?

For many in the liturgical tradition of spirituality, it is
Christian common prayer which allows us to turn human
dying into a Christian vocation. Karl Rahner writes:

> If we have been given the vocation and grace to die with
> Christ, then the everyday and banal occurrence which we
> call human death . . . has been elevated to a place among
> God's mysteries . . . For if we understand death as
> supremely the state of abandonment to God in which we
> fall into the hands of the eternal God, then we have
> already understood and endured death itself.'[37]

Death has many faces. There is the untimely death of a child
or a young parent; there is the painful death of the chronically
ill; death may come suddenly by accident or by a person's own
hand; it may be something we move into quietly and peacefully,
or something we struggle against with every fibre of our being.
Whatever the shape of death, and in whatever way we arrive
at it, it is the one certainty of our lives. Because this is true,
Dag Hammarskjold's advice is perennially sound: 'Do not seek
death. Death will find you. But seek the road which makes
death a fulfilment.'[38]

The liturgical tradition of Christian spirituality invites us to see the liturgy as the primary resource for seeking that road to fulfilment. As one contemporary representative of the liturgical tradition says:

> If we were to learn from the celebration of the paschal mystery to surrender our lives totally to God in Christ, the death of the Christian would be but the further and final rehearsal of a pattern learnt in life and practiced over and over again in a lifetime of liturgical participation ... for those who have learnt from the prayers and rituals of the Christian liturgy to let go of all that we cling to in order to save ourselves from the void, the final surrender of death will be a familiar and joyous sacrifice.[39]

In our own baptism and the baptism of others, in liturgical lament, in the Lord's Supper, in the rites of burial, we are given the opportunity to come to terms with the reality of death. We are allowed to contemplate both the mercy and the judgement of God; we are enabled to forge a relationship with eternity as we forge a relationship with the eternal God. In our sense of solidarity with those who have gone before us, forged at the font and the table and the grave, we recognise the truth in the words of Paul to the Church in Rome:

> We do not live to ourselves and we do not die to ourselves. If we live, we live to the Lord, and if we die, we die to the Lord; so then, whether we live or whether we die, we are the Lord's. For to this end Christ died and lived again, so that he might be the Lord of both the living and the dead. (Romans 14:7–9)

NOTES

1. WHAT IS LITURGICAL SPIRITUALITY?

1. *Confessions*, 7:10, tr. F. J. Sheed (New York: Sheed and Ward, 1943).
2. Alexander Schmemann, *Of Water and the Spirit* (New York: St Vladimir's Seminary Press, 1974), p. 12.
3. Gabriel Braso OSB, *Liturgical Spirituality*, tr. L. Doyle (Collegeville MN: Liturgical Press, 1960), p. 163.
4. In this volume the term 'liturgy' includes all forms of intentional public, common prayer, whatever its form or manner of celebration. This means that the silent Quaker Meeting and the Liturgy of Saint Basil and Anglican Morning Prayer are all equally considered to be within the general category 'liturgy'.
5. Braso, *Liturgical Spirituality*, p. 178.
6. Braso, *Liturgical Spirituality*, p. 179.
7. Anonymous sermon, 1662; cited in P. More and F. Cross, *Anglicanism* (London: SPCK, 1935), p. 179.
8. Augustine, *Confessions*, 9:6, tr. Sheed, p. 193.
9. John Chrysostom, *Homily on Matthew*, 82.4–6. You can see this point of view also reflected in Tertullian: 'To such a degree is the flesh the pivot of salvation, that since by it the soul becomes linked with God, it is the flesh which makes possible the soul's election to God. For example, the flesh is washed that the soul may be consecrated; the flesh is signed [with the cross] that the soul too may be protected; the flesh is overshadowed by the imposition of hands that the soul may be illuminated by the Spirit; the flesh feeds on the Body and Blood of Christ so that the soul may be replete with God. There is then no possibility of these, which the work associates, being divided in wages.' *On the Resurrection of the Body*, 8.
10. *Constitution on the Sacred Liturgy* (*Sacrosanctum Concilium*), paragraph 14, in Walter Abbot (ed.), *Documents of Vatican II* (New York: Herder and Herder, 1966).
11. *Toys and Reasons: Stages in the Ritualization of Experience* (Toronto: McLeod, 1972), p. 49.
12. Thus, a contemporary representative of the tradition can write: 'To

touch Jesus, we must not avoid rituals or try to circumvent them, but go through them to the reality of his Presence. Ritual as a discipline is meant to sensitize our faculties to the sacredness of all reality.' Thomas Keating, *The Mystery of Christ* (New York: Farrar, Straus and Giroux, 1977), p. 3.

13. Gregory of Nyssa, 'On the Baptism of Christ: a homily for the Feast of Lights' in Thomas Finn, *Early Christian Baptism and the Catechumenate: West and East Syria* (Collegeville MN: Michael Glazier/ Liturgical Press, 1992), pp. 65–6.

14. George Herbert, *The Church Porch* (stanza 67) in John N. Wall Jr. (ed.), *George Herbert: The Country Parson / The Temple*, Classics of Western Spirituality (New York: Paulist Press, 1989), p. 135.

15. Anonymous, *The New Whole Duty of Man* (1747) (London: W. Bent, 1853), p. 166.

16. Rufus Jones, 'What does prayer mean' in Harry Emerson Fosdick (ed.), *Rufus Jones Speaks to Our Times: An Anthology* (New York: Macmillan, 1952), p. 168. Jones goes on to say: 'Worship . . . is like love, and therefore it draws together and unites. Worship is not theory, it is not speculation; it is not thinking; it is not talking – it is discovery, adoration, joy, peace, communion, fellowship. The roots of our life – our real life – lie in this subsoil of our innermost being. We need to feed and fructify this deeper buried region, and to liberate its energies. That is what genuine worship does. It opens the avenues of the interior life and lets the spiritual currents from beyond us flow in and circulate about the roots of our being' (p. 169).

17. Braso, *Liturgical Spirituality*, p. 222.

18. Braso, *Liturgical Spirituality*, p. 177.

19. George Herbert, for example, advises the 'country parson' to exhort parishioners to avail themselves of the lessons the liturgy has to teach, in this case the lessons to be learned from the experience of baptism: '[The parson] adviseth all to call to mind their Baptism often . . . certainly it is the safest course for Christians to meditate on their Baptism often (being the first step into their great and glorious calling) and upon what terms, and with what vows, they were baptized.' George Herbert, *The Country Parson*, Chapter XXII (Classics, p. 85).

20. *Sermon on the Eucharistic Assembly.*

21. Georges Florovsky, *Prayer: Private and Corporate*, p. 3. Almost all representatives of the tradition make this point at one time or another. A German Lutheran, reflecting on liturgical prayer in the midst of the experience of war, puts it this way: 'Man needs formula as a model, to practice saying his own prayer as an answer to the God who speaks to him, just the same way as a child learns . . . In formulas which are common to all Christians . . . the borders of prayer widen out, and it becomes a gift offered by brothers together.' Emmanuel von Severus, 'Dem heiligen Benedikt heute begegnen' (in

Erbe und Auftrag, Beuron, 56 (1980), pp. 293–4; cited in George Guiver, *Company of Voices: Daily Prayer and the People of God* (New York: Pueblo, 1988), p. 25.

22. Augustine, *Selected Writings* (New York: Paulist, 1968), p. 233. Others within the tradition say the liturgy is an effective teacher because it is able to make the mystery of God sensible to human faculties. In the *Celestial Heirarchy* 2: 1–3, Dionysius the Areopagite speaks of those who are newly baptised into the community of faith: 'This initiation in the sacred symbols of divine regeneration contains nothing unbecoming or irreverent, nor does it contain any sensible image, *but reflects through natural images suitable to human capacities enigmas of contemplation worthy of God*' (emphasis added).

23. William Beveredge, seventeenth-century Bishop of St Asaph, 'A sermon on the excellency and usefulness of the Book of Common Prayer', 1681–2, cited in J. Robert Wright (ed.), *Prayer Book Spirituality* (New York: Church Hymnal Corporation, 1989), pp. 72ff.

24. Braso, *Liturgical Spirituality*, p. 98.

25. Aidan Kavanagh, *On Liturgical Theology* (New York: Pueblo, 1984), pp. 153–4.

26. Hymn 71 v. 1 'Hymns on the Lord's Supper' in J. Rattenbury (ed.), *The Eucharistic Hymns of John and Charles Wesley* (London: Epworth, 1948). The Wesleys make this point over and over again. In his famous sermon 'On the Means of Grace', John Wesley says that 'the outward signs, words, actions' are the 'ordinary channels whereby [God] might convey to men preventing, justifying, or sanctifying grace'. And later, 'The sure and general rule for all who groan for the salvation of God is this – whenever opportunity serves, use all means God has ordained. For who knows in which God will meet thee with grace that bringeth salvation?'

27. *Constitution on the Sacred Liturgy*, paragraph 61.

28. See Ann Bedford Ulanov, *Primary Speech* (Atlanta: John Knox Press, 1982).

29. Evelyn Underhill, *School of Charity* (New York: Longmans Green, 1954), p. 94.

30. Kavanagh, *On Liturgical Theology*, pp. 87–8.

31. 'The Holy Communion', line 22, in Herbert, *Country Parson*, p. 167.

32. Gordon Lathrop, *Holy Things* (Minneapolis MN: Fortress Press, 1993), pp. 172–3.

33. Duffy, *Real Presence* (San Francisco: Harper and Row, 1982), p. 176.

34. Ann Savage, (ed.), *Anchoritic Spirituality: Ancrene Wisse and Associated Works*, Classics of Western Spirituality (New York: Paulist Press, 1991), p. 156.

35. *Homilae in Johannem* 46.

36. Robert Barclay, *Apology for the True Christian Divinity*, Proposition xi, section 7 (London, 1678), p. 240.

37. Nornan Pittenger, *Life as Eucharist* (Grand Rapids: Eerdmans, 1979), p. 48.

38. Kathleen Norris, 'Stop making sense' in 'A symposium on writing spirituality', in *Manoa* 7:1 (Summer 1995), p. 115.

39. Alexander Schmemann, *For the Life of the World* (New York: Saint Vladimir's Seminary Press, 1973), p. 48.

40. This from the admonition of the late Norman Pittenger: 'Inevitably and inescapably, once we permit ourselves to be molded and built up in the liturgical life of the Church, our whole being becomes "liturgical".' Pittenger, *Life*, p. 55.

41. Pittenger, *Life*, p. 48.

42. Schmemann, *Life of the World*, p. 16. Schmemann uses this book to expand upon and rework Feuerbach's aphorism.

43. Augustine, *Sermon* 272. Likewise he says in *Sermon* 265: 'These things, my brothers and sisters, are called sacraments for the reason that in them one thing is seen, but another is understood. That which is seen has physical appearance, that which is understood has spiritual fruit. If then you wish to understand the Body of Christ, listen to the Apostle as he says to the faithful, "You are the Body of Christ and his members." (1 Corinthians 12:27). If, therefore, you are the Body of Christ and his members, your mystery has been placed on the Lord's table, you receive your mystery.'

44. A good example is British Methodist Geoffrey Wainwright, whose groundbreaking works *Doxology* (New York: Oxford University Press, 1980) and *Eucharist and Eschatology* (London: Epworth, 1971) set up a usable methodology for the discipline of liturgical theology.

45. Over and over again we read in journals, spiritual autobiographies, and affirmations of faith words similar to those of a Scottish Methodist, writing in the middle of this century, of his experience of singing the hymn 'O Love That Wilt Not Let Me Go': 'At a time of great spiritual darkness, when God, Christ, and Heaven seemed to have gone out of my Life, and neither sun nor stars in many days appeared, after months of hopeless misery of mind, I heard this hymn sung in a little country chapel. The first two lines haunted me for weeks, and at last brought light and comfort to my dark soul.' Cited in Kenneth Young, *Chapel* (London: Eyre Methuen, 1972), p. 75. How reminiscent of poet/pastor George Herbert's address 'To Church Music': 'But if I travel in your company,/You know the way to heaven's door'!

46. A brief example will suffice in this regard. Because of their nearly universal belief that liturgy was indeed a great spiritual resource, all of the Protestant reformers of the sixteenth century argued that the liturgy should be in a language that the people could understand. One advisor to Pope Leo X, Paris de Grassi, urged the Pope to make a swift response to 'all those who think that religious ceremonies should be made accessible to the majority of people,' because he believed that the authority of the papacy depended in large measure

on the reverent attitude of the rich and powerful toward the liturgy. 'In effect,' de Grassi writes in 1516, 'they believe that the pontiffs are not mortal men, but a species of gods on earth . . . they are captivated with an admiration without limits when they contemplate the ceremonies . . . [which appear] to include some divine features. But, if the secrets of worship are revealed and the ceremonies made accessible, there will result immediately a loss of prestige.' Although de Grassi would probably share with the liturgical tradition the conviction that the liturgy has the power to shape the heart, mind and soul of the believer, his use of the liturgy strictly as a power-political tool puts him outside of the tradition.
47. Gerald Vann, *Morals and Man* (London: Collins, 1959), p. 102.

2. REVEALING OUR IDENTITY AND VOCATION

1. 'Either-Or' in *Provinces: Poems 1987–1991* (New York: Ecco, 1991), p. 37.
2. *Constitution on the Sacred Liturgy*, paragraph 2.
3. Robert Taft, 'What does liturgy do?' in *Worship*, 66:3 (May 1992), pp. 209–10.
4. Charles Davis, 'Ghetto or desert?' in *Studia Liturgica*, 7.2–3 (1970), p. 14.
5. Lord Lawson, cited in Rupert Davies, *History of the Methodist Church in Great Britain*, II (London: Epworth, 1965), p. 105.
6. Martin Thornton, *English Spirituality* (London: SPCK, 1963), pp. 99–100.
7. *The Idea of Lyric* (Berkeley: University of California Press, 1982), p. 177.
8. *The Memory of Old Jack* (New York: Harcourt, Brace, Jovanovich, 1974).
9. Braso, *Liturgical Spirituality*, p. 168.
10. *Pastoral Constitution on the Church in the Modern World* (*Gaudium et Spes*), 35.
11. Alexander Schmemann, *Of Water and the Spirit*, p. 139. Another representative of the liturgical tradition says something very similar about the function of naming in the establishment of human identity: '[T]o give a name is to give life . . . To name is to transform; to strengthen the vulnerable and encourage the fainthearted; to locate those who are displaced, or as yet unplaced, or who stand in danger of losing their way in the terrifying new world that lies before them.' Roger Grainger, *The Message of the Rite: The Significance of Christian Rites of Passage* (Cambridge: Lutterworth Press, 1988), p. 50.
12. *The Gospel According to Philip*, 86.
13. Duffy, *Real Presence*, p. 39.
14. Robert Coles, *Spiritual Life of Children* (Boston: Houghton Mifflin, 1980), p. 136.

15. Schmemann, *Water and Spirit*, p. 152.

16. *Memra*, 7: 179–60.

17. Martin Luther, *The Bapylonian Captivity of the Church* in Hans Hillerbrand (ed.), *Luther's Works*, vol. 36 (Minneapolis: Fortress Press, 1964), pp. 67–8. Hereinafter cited as *LW*.

18. *Baptismal Homily*, 16.24.

19. Vincent Donovan, *Christianity Rediscovered* (Maryknoll NY: Orbis, 1981), p. 97.

20. John Scott, cited in J. H. Overton, *Life in the English Church* (London: Longmans Green, 1885), p. 273.

21. Maxwell Johnson, 'Baptismal spirituality', *Worship*, 71:6 (November 1997), p. 492.

22. Cyril of Jerusalem, *Mystagogical Catechesis, 4* in Daniel Sheerin (ed.), *The Eucharist*, Message of the Fathers of the Church, 7 (Wilmington DE: Michael Glazier, 1986).

23. Alexander Schmemann, *Sacraments and Orthodoxy* (New York: Herder and Herder, 1965), p. 93.

24. Duffy, *Real Presence*, p. 124. Anglican bishop and theologian John V. Taylor says something very similar when he writes: 'John had said; "he will baptize you with the Holy Spirit" (Mark 1:8). The point about the Christian's baptism is that he remains in that element into which he is baptized – "into Christ" (Galatians 3:27); "in the Holy Spirit" (Acts 11:16); "into union with Christ Jesus, into his death" (Romans 6:3). He does not leave those waters behind, but lives on in their meaning ... We may, then, and indeed we must, allow the awesome archetypal resonances of the water symbol to fill out our understanding of baptism and of that life in the Spirit which it represents.' *The Go-Between God* (London: SCM Press, 1972), p. 45.

25. Schmemann, *Life of the World*, p. 61.

26. Clement of Alexandria, *Paedagogus*, 1: 42–3.

27. Paul Connerton, *How Societies Remember* (Cambridge: Cambridge University Press, 1988), p. 102.

28. Raimundo Panikkar, *Worship and Secular Man* (Maryknoll NY: Orbis, 1973), p. 59.

29. Stephanie Paulsell, 'Honoring the Body' in Dorothy Bass (ed.), *Practicing Our Faith* (San Francisco: Josey Bass), p. 22.

30. David Jones, *Epoch and Artist: Selected Writings* (London: Faber and Faber, 1959), p. 167.

31. Bernard Häring, *The Eucharist and Our Everyday Life* (New York: Seabury /Crossroad, 1979), p. 92.

32. Schmemann, *Sacraments and Orthodoxy*, p. 108.

33. Schmemann, *Life of the World*, pp. 89–90.

34. Taylor, *Go-Between God*, p. 69.

35. B. Kilroy, 'Letter to the Editor', *Church Times* (6/6/97), p. 8.

36. Walter Hilton, *The Scale of Perfection*, part II, ed. E. Underhill (London: Watkins, 1948), p. 42.

37. Tilden Edwards, *Sabbath Time* (New York: Seabury Press, 1982), p. 74.
38. Lluis Duch, 'The experience and symbolism of time' in *The Times of Celebration* (*Concilium* 142) p. 26.
39. Schmemann, *Life of the World*, p. 45.
40. Søren Kierkegaard, *Purity of Heart is to Will One Thing* (New York: Harper and Row, 1948), p. 198.
41. Walter Brueggemann, *The Bible and the Post-Modern imagination* (London: SCM Press, 1993), p. 49.
42. Thomas Kelly, *Testament of Devotion* (London: Harper Brothers, 1941), pp. 41–2.
43. Kelly, *Testament of Devotion*.
44. Clement of Alexandria, *Protrepticus*, 1.4.4.
45. 'Holy, holy, holy Lord, God of power and might; heaven and earth are full of your glory. Hosanna in the highest.'
46. Cyril of Jerusalem, *Mystagogical Catechesis 5* (emphasis added).
47. Don Saliers, 'Singing our lives' in Bass (ed.), *Practicing Our Faith*, p. 180.
48. Augustine, *Treatise on John*, 65:1–7.
49. Deitrich Bonhoeffer, *Life Together*, tr. John Doberstein (New York; Harper and Brothers, 1954), pp. 57–8.
50. Pittenger, *Life*, p. 82.

3. ESTABLISHING COMMUNITY

1. *Didascalia*, II:59:1–3.
2. *Mystagogical Catechesis* in *Maximus the Confessor: Selected Writings*, tr. G. Berthold (New York: Paulist Press, 1979), p. 206.
3. *Mystagogical Catechesis*, p. 206.
4. *Homily on Matthew* in P. Schaff (ed.), *A Select Library of Nicene and Post-Nicene Fathers of the Christian Church* (Grand Rapids MI: Eerdmans, 1956).
5. *Homily on Matthew*.
6. London Yearly Meeting of the Society of Friends, *Christian Faith and Practice* (London: London Yearly Meeting, 1925), p. 237.
7. Augustine, *Sermon Wolfenbuttel*, 7.
8. *Didache*, 8:4.
9. *LW*, 35, 58.
10. John Chrysostom, *Sermon on the Betrayal of Judas*. Cyprian of Carthage makes the same sort of point, using the words of the Lord's Prayer as his example: 'Before all things the teacher of peace and master of unity would not have prayer to be made singly and individually; so that when one prays, he does not pray for himself alone. For we say not "*My* Father which art in heaven", nor "give *me* this day *my* daily bread" ... Our prayer is public and common; and when we

pray, we pray not for one, but for the whole people, because the whole people are one.' Cyprian, *On the Lord's Prayer*, 8.

11. William Gladstone, 'O Lead my Blindness By the Hand', *The English Hymnal* (1933), hymn 322.

12. Martin Luther, 'The Blessed Sacrament . . . and the Brotherhoods' in *LW*, 35, 51.

13. Juan Segundo, *Sacraments Today*, vol. IV, *A Theology for Artisans of a New Humanity* (Maryknoll NY: Orbis, 1973), p. 91.

14. Mark Searle, 'Serving the Lord with justice' in Mark Searle (ed.), *Liturgy and Social Justice* (Collegeville: Liturgical Press, 1980), p. 32.

15. Nathan Mitchell, 'The Amen Corner', *Worship*, 66:2 (March 1992), p. 183.

16. Searle, *Liturgy and Social Justice*, p. 24.

17. Searle, *Liturgy and Social Justice*, p. 24.

18. Searle, *Liturgy and Social Justice*, p. 24.

19. *Didascalia*, 12.

20. Kavanaugh, *On Liturgical Theology*, p. 75.

21. David Newman, *Worship as Praise and Empowerment* (New York: Pilgrim Press, 1988), p. 148.

22. Augustine, *Sermon* 340.1.

23. Aidan Kavanagh, 'Unbegun and unfinished revisited' in Maxwell Johnson, *The Rites of Christian Initiation* (Collegeville MN: Pueblo, 1998), pp. 267–8.

24. Robert Hovda, cited in Walton, 'Current prophetic challenge to liturgists', p. 105.

25. Evelyn Underhill, *The School of Charity* (London: Longmans, 1934), p. 93.

26. This instruction to join with the heavenly host in praise of God is usually followed by the hymn in Isaiah 6:3: 'Holy, holy, holy Lord, God of power and might; Heaven and earth are full of your glory; Hosanna in the Highest!'

27. Schmemann, *Sacraments and Orthodoxy*, p. 30.

28. *The Hermitage Within* (London: Darton, Longman and Todd, 1974), p. 29.

29. Henry Scott Holland, *Sacramental Values* (1917), cited in Donald Gray, *Earth and Altar* (London: Alcuin Club, 1986), p. 126. Holland was founder of the Christian Social Union.

30. Newman, *Worship*, p. 91.

31. Newman, *Worship*, p. 117.

32. Schmemann, *Life of the World*, p. 25.

33. Richard Fenn, *Liturgies and Trials*, (New York: Pilgrim Press, 1982), p. 28.

34. Paul Bradshaw, *Two Ways of Praying* (London: SPCK, 1995), p. 107.

35. Quoted in Schmemann, *Life of the World*, p. 37.

36. Tissa Balasuriya, *The Eucharist and Human Liberation* (Maryknoll NY: Orbis, 1979), p. 164.

37. Michael Ramsey, *Introducing the Christian Faith* (London: SCM Press, 1961), p. 81.
38. Newman, *Worship*, pp. 34–5.
39. Alexander Schmemann, *Great Lent* (New York: St Vladimir's Seminary Press, 1974), p. 99.

4. LOCATING OURSELVES IN TIME AND SPACE

1. Schmemann, *Sacraments and Orthodoxy*, p. 59.
2. Adrian Nocent, *The Liturgical Year*, vol. 1, tr. Matthew O'Connell (Collegeville: Liturgical Press, 1977), p. 15.
3. Leo the Great, *Sermon* 26, 'On the Feast of the Nativity IV', 12:137.
4. Herbert, 'Lent' in Classics, pp. 205–6.
5. Newman, *Worship*, pp. 108–9.
6. Keating, *Mystery of Christ*, p. 79.
7. See, for example, Wainwright, *Eucharist and Eschatology*.
8. Bonhoeffer, *Life Together*, p. 53.
9. Keating, *Mystery of Christ*, p. 93.
10. Abraham Joshua Heschel, *The Sabbath* (New York: Farrar, Straus and Giroux, 1977), pp. 216–17.
11. Larry Hoffman, 'Shabbat', *Liturgy*, 8:1 (1989), p. 21.
12. *I Clement*, 24:1–3.
13. Herbert, 'Sunday' in Classics, p. 192.
14. Heschel, *Sabbath*, p. 218.
15. Luther goes on to say: 'Days and times should not control Christians. Rather Christians freely exercise control over days and times.' Cited in Alan Jones, *Passion for Pilgrimage* (San Francisco: Harper and Row, 1989), p. 69.
16. George Steiner, *Real Presences* (Chicago: Chicago University Press, 1989), pp. 231–2.
17. Dorothy Bass, 'Keeping Sabbath' in Bass (ed.), *Practicing our Faith*, p. 88.
18. Margaret Visser, *Rituals of Dinner* (New York: Penguin, 1992), pp. 36–7.
19. Schmemann, *Life of the World*, p. 63.
20. *I Clement*, 24.1.
21. *I Clement*, 24.1.
22. Philip Pfatteicher, *Liturgical Spirituality* (Valley Forge PA: Trinity Press International, 1997), p. 38.
23. Sister Thekla, *The Service of Vespers: Prayers of the Day* (Library of Orthodox Thinking, nos 3 and 4, 1976 and 1977). Cited in, Guiver *Company of Voices*, pp. 15–16.
24. Pfatteicher, *Liturgical Spirituality*, p. 108.
25. Laurence Hull Stookey, *Calendar: Christ's Time for the Church* (Nashville TN: Abingdon Press, 1996), p. 150.
26. Jones, *Pilgrimage*, p. 69.

27. Mitchell, 'The Amen Corner', p. 264.
28. Jones, *Pilgrimage*, p. 1.
29. Cited in Pfatteicher, *Pilgrimage*, pp. 117–18. A contemporary representative of the tradition, Methodist Laurence Stookey, says something very similar: 'By observing Christ's time for the Church, year in and year out, we make our pilgrim journey – not as if walking in circles on the same plot of ground, but as if ascending a spiral staircase. Annually we go around in what may seem at first to be the same pattern; but gradually it dawns on us that always we see where we have been from a greater height, and by virtue of the increasing elevation we can look farther across the landscape of faith to gain a better perspective on God's gracious design and on our place within it. Thereby we come to believe more confidently, Lord's Day by Lord's Day and Pasch by Pasch, that we, too, will be numbered with the saints in glory everlasting.' *Calendar*, p. 136.
30. Stookey, *Calendar*, p. 17.
31. Marianne Sawicki, *Seeing the Lord: Resurrection in Early Christian Perspective* (Minneapolis: Fortress Press, 1994), pp. 335–6.
32. Milton J. Crumm, 'Our approach to the church year: chronological or eschatological?' *Worship*, 51 (January 1977), pp. 24–5.
33. Keating, *Mystery of Christ*, p. 79.
34. Keating, *Mystery of Christ*, p. 79.
35. Pfatteicher, *Liturgical Spirituality*, p. 141.
36. *Sacred and Profane* (New York: Harcourt, Brace, World, 1959), p. 25.
37. *Sermon* 336, 1.6.
38. Pfatteicher, *Liturgical Spirituality*, p. 167.
39. Pfatteicher, *Liturgical Spirituality*, p. 162.
40. John Jewel, 'The Reply to Harding's Answer' in J. Ayre (ed.), *The Works of John Jewel* (Cambridge: Parker Society, 1887), p. 660.
41. See, for example, Margaret Miles, *Image as Insight* (Boston: Beacon, 1985).
42. 'You are not here to verify, Instruct yourself, or inform curiosity/ Or carry report; You are here to kneel/Where prayer has been valid . . .'. *The Four Quartets: Little Gidding* in *The Complete Poems and Plays, 1909–1950* (New York: Harcourt, Brace and Co., 1952), p. 139.
43. 'Church-going' in *Collected Poems* (London: Farrar, Straus and Giroux, 1988), pp. 97–8.
44. Guiver, *Company of Voices*, p. 37.
45. Origen, 'Concerning the place of prayer' in *First Principles*, Book I:3:4–5.
46. K. M. George, *The Silent Roots* (Geneva: WCC, 1998), p. xi.
47. Origen, 'Concerning the place of prayer'.
48. Cuthbert, Bishop of Coventry, in Basil Spence, *Phoenix at Coventry* (London: Collins Fontana, 1962), p. 11.
49. *Second Homily on the Cross of the Lord*.
50. Herbert, 'Sunday', lines 15–21.

51. Theodore of Mopsuestia, *Homily*, 15.15.
52. Theodore of Mopsuestia, *Homily*, 15.20.
53. Pfatteicher, *Liturgical Spirituality*, p. 173.

5. LIVING RESPONSIBLY

1. Frederick Denison Maurice, *The Prayerbook* (Cambridge: Macmillan, 1852), p. xi.
2. K. E. Kirk, *Some Principles of Moral Theology* (London: Longmans Green, 1920), p. 221.
3. Ignatius, *Letter to the Smyrneans*, 13:1.
4. 'Ancrene Wisse' in *Anchoritic Spirituality*, p. 147.
5. *Anchoritic Spirituality*, p. 146.
6. Pseudo-Dionysius, *The Ecclesiastical Hierarchy*, 401A:5.
7. These words, or words very like them, would have been a part of the baptismal rite that such people as John Chrysostom, Cyril of Jerusalem, Gregory of Nyssa and Theodore of Mopsuestia would have known. Similar formulae appear in nearly all ancient rites, both East and West. See Thomas M. Finn (ed.), *Early Christian Baptism and the Catechumenate: West and East Syria* (Collegeville MN: Michael Glazier/Liturgical Press, 1992) for the ancient commentaries and liturgical homilies on these rites.
8. *Homily on 1 Corinthians*, 27.8.
9. Augustine, *Sermon 227*.
10. *Sermon on the Betrayal of Judas*. Augustine makes much the same point, reflecting on the singing of the Easter hymns: 'Sing to the Lord a new song. Look, you tell me, "I am singing!" Yes indeed, you are singing. You are singing clearly, I hear you. But make sure that your life does not contradict your words. Sing with your voices, your lips, and your lives. Sing to the Lord a new song ... If you desire to praise him, then live what you express. Live good lives and you yourselves will be his praise.' *Sermon 34*, 5–6.
11. Bernard Häring, puts it this way: 'If we have celebrated with heartfelt joy and gratitude, we shall understand that the kiss of peace, received from Christ and shared among the participants, issues in a life that continues to reflect this experience ... Reconciled, we shall work for reconciliation; graced we shall be gracious – ever more true and efficacious image of the love of God, the peace of Christ, the rallying power of the Holy Spirit. The Eucharist – praise and thanksgiving – will always and everywhere be the leitmotif that gives direction and coherence to all our thoughts, desires, words and actions ... [as we] live this spirit of gratitude towards God and our neighbour and thus spread the peace of the Gospel.' *Eucharist*, pp. 91–2.
12. Orthodox theologian Alexander Schmemann adds: 'It is no accident that the story of the Fall is centered on food, on hunger, on food received "non-eucharistically," that is not as a gift from God. It is

taken with disregard of God. Food "whose eating was condemned to be communion only with itself alone, and not with God." ' *Life of the World*, p. 17.

13. Duffy, *Real Presence*, p. 9.
14. Duffy, *Real Presence*, p. 3.
15. Amos 5:21–24.
16. F. M. Garrett, *The Church Reformer*, vol. viii, no. 11 (November 1889), p. 252, cited in Donald Gray, *Earth and Altar* (London: Alcuin, 1986), p. 120.
17. Robert Ledogar CFMS, 'Table prayers and Eucharist: questions from the social sciences' in Herman Schmidt (ed.), *Concilium 52: Prayer and Community* (New York: Herder and Herder, 1970), p. 116. In his well-known book *The Eucharist and Human Liberation* (Maryknoll NY: Orbis, 1979), Tissa Balasuryia, makes much the same point: 'The eucharistic bread is a common meal for all, but bread in the world is a commodity for trade. In the eucharistic ideal, land is for common use; in the system of nation states land is for the successful conquerors. The eucharist gives a priority to persons; in international relations, power and profit prevail . . . The eucharist is the sacrament of unity, it must also be the sacrament of world justice' (p. 142).
18. See Searle, *Liturgy*, p. 28.
19. Leech, *True Prayer*, p. 102.
20. John Howard Yoder, *The Politics of Jesus* (Grand Rapids: Eerdmans, 1972), p. 66.
21. Gordon Lathrop, 'The Eucharist as a "hungry feast" and the appropriateness of our want', *Living Worship*, 13 (November 1977), p. 17. Raimundo Panikkar speaks in another way of the challenges of this 'hungry feast': 'The great challenge today is to convert the sacred bread into real bread, the liturgical peace into political peace, the worship of the Creator into reverence for the Creation, the Christian praying community into an authentic human fellowship.' 'Man as ritual being', *Chicago Studies*, 16 (1977), p. 27.
22. Searle, 'Serving the Lord with justice', p. 28. He continues: 'Like the Word of God in history, the liturgy is the revelation of God's justice in both event and word, cutting into human life both as good news and denunciation. It proclaims and realizes the saving presence in the world, and enables us to realize where this is happening even outside the liturgy. Celebrating the liturgy should train us to recognize justice and injustice when we see it . . . In saying "Amen" to the justice of God proclaimed in the liturgy, we are implicitly saying "Anathema" to all that fails to measure up to that justice.'
23. Segundo Galilea, '¿A los Pobres se le anuncia el evangelio?', cited in Rafael Avila, *Worship and Politics* (Maryknoll NY: Orbis, 1981), p. 84.
24. 'For the Time Being'.
25. *Opusculum*, 7.

26. Rowan Williams, *Resurrection* (New York: Morehouse Barlow, 1977), p. 52.
27. *Concilium*, 97, p. 64.
28. Jones, *Pilgrimage*, p. 4. This requires the kind of radical honesty that the liturgy invites us into. As another contemporary representative of the tradition puts it: 'The imagery that lies at the heart of worship is used for purposes of encounter rather than evasion. Liturgy is a confrontation with the underlying truth of human being. It is very important to realize that the special, "world-of-its-own" quality of the rite is to do with concentration rather than evasion.' Grainger, *Message of the Rite*, p. 37.
29. Jürgen Moltmann, *Theology of Play* (San Francisco: Harper and Row, 1972), p. 45.
30. *Against Latomus* (1521); *LW* 32: 227.
31. Cyril, *Catechetical Lecture*, 16:12.
32. *Institutes*, IV: XVII, 10, *The Institutes of the Christian Religion* (Library of Christian Classics), p. 1370.
33. Theophilus of Alexandria, *Sermon on the Mystical Supper*.
34. Keating, *Mystery of Christ*, p. 37.
35. Jones, *Pilgrimage*, p. 85.
36. Roland Perry Smith, 'Bethany: memories and visions', *Brethren Life and Thought*, 39 (Winter 1994), pp. 34–5.
37. Alfred North Whitehead, *Science and the Modern World* (New York: Macmillan, 1925), pp. 268–9.
38. Brueggemann, *Bible*, p. 25.
39. *Constitution on the Sacred Liturgy*, para. 93.
40. Merle D. Strenge, 'Ecclesiology and the Lord's Supper: the memorial meal of a peaceable community' in *The Lord's Supper: Believers Church Perspectives*, ed. Dale R. Stoffer (Scottdale PA: Herald Press, 1996), p. 128.
41. See, for example, Timothy Ware, describing the worship of the Orthodox Church: 'Worship, in the Orthodox Church, is nothing else than "heaven on earth." The Holy Liturgy is something that embraces two worlds at once, for both in heaven and earth the Liturgy is one and the same – one altar, one sacrifice, one presence. In every place of worship, however humble its outward appearance, as the faithful gather . . . they are taken up into the "heavenly place"; in every place of worship when the Holy Sacrifice is offered, not merely the local congregation is present, but the Church universal – the saints, the angels, the Mother of God, Christ himself.' *The Orthodox Church* (New York: Penguin, 1980), p. 270.
42. Pittenger, *Life*, p. 69.
43. Lawrence Hoffman, 'Welcoming Shabbat: the power of metaphor', *Liturgy* 8:1 (1989), p. 23.
44. Kavanagh, *On Liturgical Theology*, pp. 153–4.

6. NEGOTIATING SICKNESS, DYING AND DEATH

1. David Power, 'The sacrament of anointing: open questions' in Mary Collins and David N. Power (eds.), *Pastoral Care of the Sick* (*Concilium*, 1991/2), pp. 103–4.
2. Susan Sontag, *Illness as Metaphor* (New York: Farrar, Straus and Giroux, 1978), p. 9.
3. Simone Weil, *Waiting for God* (New York: Putnam, 1951), p. 64.
4. M. Jennifer Glenn, 'Sickness and symbol: the promise of the future', *Worship*, 54:5 (September 1980), p. 397.
5. Power, 'Anointing', pp. 103–4.
6. Power, 'Anointing', p. 104.
7. Cited in Charles Gusmer, *The Ministry of Healing* (London: Alcuin Club, 1972), p. 42. Ephrem of Syria, speaking of the oil of anointing, says that 'Christ has many facets, and the oil acts as a mirror to them all; from whatever angle I look at the oil, Christ looks out at me from it.' Translated by Sebastian Brock, *The Harp of the Spirit: Eighteen Poems of Saint Ephrem* (London, Fellowship of Saint Alban and Saint Sergius, 1983).
8. Robert Duggan, 'The new rite of the Anointing of the sick', *Liturgy*, 25:2 (1980), p. 14.
9. Mark Searle, *Liturgy Made Simple* (Collegeville MN: Liturgical Press, 1981), p. 67.
10. Schmemann, *Sacraments and Orthodoxy*, p. 128.
11. Ireneus, *Adversus Heresies*, 12:6
12. Antonio Mongillo, 'Healing' in William Bassett and Peter Huizing (eds.), *Experience of the Spirit* (*Concilium*, 99), p. 126.
13. *Paedagogus*, I:VI. 46–7. Clement is referring here to the practice of adding some of the communion bread to the wine at communion for the purpose of more easily giving communion to those debilitated by sickness.
14. Cited in Braso, *Liturgical Spirituality*, p. 35.
15. Ignatius of Antioch, *Letter to the Ephesians*, 20: 2.
16. As Baron Frederich von Hugel says, 'In suffering we are very near to God'.
17. Mitchell, 'The Amen Corner', p. 563.
18. John 9:12
19. Matthew 9:5; Luke 5:18; Mark 2:9 (NRSV)
20. Power, 'Anointing', p. 102.
21. Although this is a commonplace observation, it was brought to my attention recently in a particularly forceful way. Reading a funeral industry journal, I came across an advertisement from a manufacturer of a high-priced line of coffins which were described as providing the deceased with 'All the warmth that wood can give'.
22. Karl Rahner, 'Secular life and the sacraments', *Tablet* (6 March 1971), p. 237.

23. Braso, *Liturgical Spirituality*, p. 32.
24. *The Passion of Saint Perpetua and Saint Felicity*, 12.
25. *Catechetical Homily*, XIV:5.
26. Pfatteicher, *Liturgical Spirituality*, p. 238.
27. *LW*, 35:31
28. 'Christian Doctrine' in *The Complete Writings of Menno Simons*, tr. Leonard Verdun and John C. Wenger (Scottdale PA: Herald Press, 1956), pp. 53–154.
29. *Adversus Heresies*, IV:18.5 (see also IV:5.2).
30. ' "Principal Shairp" of Hawick', quoted in J. J. Vernon, *The Parish and Church of Hawick, 1711–1725*, The Hawick Express Reprint Series (Hawick, Scotland: The Hawick Express, n.d.), p. 7.
31. Gerhard Zerbolt of Zutphen, 'The scriptural ascents' in John van Engen (ed.), *Devotio Moderna: Basic Writings*, Classics of Western Spirituality (New York: Paulist Press, 1988), p. 278.
32. Häring, *Eucharist*, pp. 61–2.
33. Grainger, *Message of the Rite*, pp. 66–7.
34. Amy Plantinga Pauw, 'Dying well' in Bass (ed.), *Practicing our Faith*, p. 168.
35. Grainger, *Message of the Rite*, p. 30.
36. Maggie Kuhn, cited in Heinecken, 'Christian theology and aging', in William Clements (ed.), *Ministry with the Aging* (San Francisco: Harper and Row, 1981), p. 89.
37. Karl Rahner, 'On Christian dying', *Theological Investigations*, 7 (London: Darton, Longman and Todd, 1969), p. 293.
38. Hammarskjold, *Markings* (New York: Knopf, 1964), p. 136.
39. Mark Searle, *Assembly*, 3:5 (March 1979), p. 49.

SELECT BIBLIOGRAPHY

Bernstein csj, Eleanor, *Liturgy and Spirituality in Context: Perspectives on Prayer and Culture* (Collegeville MN: Liturgical Press, 1990).

Bradshaw, Paul, *Two Ways of Praying: Introducing Liturgical Spirituality* (London: SPCK, 1995).

Braso osb, Gabriel, *Liturgical Spirituality*, tr. L. Doyle (Collegeville MN: Liturgical Press, 1960).

Collins osb, Mary, *Contempletive Participation: Sacrosanctum Concilium Twenty-five Years Later* (Collegeville MN: Liturgical Press, 1990).

Constitution on the Sacred Liturgy (Sacrosanctum Concilium) in *The Documents of Vatican II*, ed. Walter M. Abbot sj (The America Press, 1966).

Crosby, Michael H., *Thy Will Be Done: Praying the Our Father as Subversive Activity* (Maryknoll NY: Orbis, 1977).

Grainger, Roger, *The Message of the Rite* (Cambridge: Lutterworth Press, 1988).

Gray, Donald, *Earth and Altar: The Evolution of the Parish Communion in the Church of England to 1945* (London: Alcuin Club, 1986).

Guiver, George, *Company of Voices: Daily Prayer and the People of God* (New York: Pueblo, 1988).

Häring, Bernard, *The Eucharist and Our Everyday Life* (New York: Seabury/Crossroad, 1979).

Irwin, Kevin, *Liturgy, Prayer, and Spirituality* (New York: Paulist Press, 1984).

Jones, Alan, *Passion for Pilgrimage* (San Francisco: Harper and Row, 1989).

Keating, Thomas, *The Mystery of Christ: The Liturgy as a Spiritual Experience* (New York: Farrar, Strauss and Giroux, 1977).

Lathrop, Gordon, *Holy Things* (Minneapolis MN: Fortress Press, 1993).

Newman, David, *Worship as Praise and Empowerment* (New York: Pilgrim Press, 1988).

Pfatteicher, Philip H., *Liturgical Spirituality* (Valley Forge PA: Trinity Press International, 1997).

Saliers, Don E., *Worship and Spirituality* (Philadelphia: Westminster Press, 1984).

Schmemann, Alexander, *Of Water and the Spirit* (New York: St Vladimir's Seminary Press, 1974).

Wagner, Mary Anthony, *The Sacred World of the Christian: Sensed in Faith* (Collegeville MN: Liturgical Press, 1993).

Wright, J. Robert, *Prayer Book Spirituality: A Devotional Companion to the Book of Common Prayer* (New York: Church Hymnal Corporation, 1989).